THE
FAIR DINKUM
COOKBOOK

THE FAIR DINKUM COOKBOOK

AUSSIE FOOD AS IT USED TO BE

BY

COLIN HESTON

INTERNATIONAL EDITION
FULL COLOUR

HARROW AND HESTON
Publishers

Australia, New York & Philadelphia

Copyright © 2020 Harrow and Heston, Publishers.

All rights reserved.

No part of this publication may be reproduced, stored in a retrieval system, or transmitted in any form or by any means, electronic, mechanical, photocopying, recording, or otherwise, without the prior permission of the publisher.

The author is grateful to Keith McKenry and *Bunyip Bush Enterprises* for permission to reproduce *At the Sign of the Ravenous Goanna*, taken from *The Spirit of the People: Modern Australian Recitations*, 1983.

International Digital Edition
ISBN: 978-0-911577-55-6

International Paperback Edition
ISBN: 978-0-911577-56-3

Library of Congress Control Number: 2020939245

Cover design by Graeme Newman. Artwork from 'A Halt. While the Billy Boils' postcard, 1910, Massey-Harris Co Ltd. Josef Lebovic collection, National Museum of Australia.

Table of Contents

1. The Aussie Way 1
2. Pie 'n Sauce and other Aussie Classics 4
3. Sandwiches and Scones 13
4. Prawns, Snags and other Barbie Delights 25
5. Fish, Chook and Rabbit 34
6. The Aussie Melting Pot 50
7. Salads 67
8. Cookies and Slices 73
9. Cakes 88
10. Desserts 103
11. Icing, Fillings and Spreads 116
12. Drinks and Drinking 120
13. Outback Cooking 129

Glossary of Indigenous Australian Foods 155

Aussie Measurements and Ingredients 157

About the Author 161

Dedicated to the Aussie mums of history who gave their lives to the kitchen

At the Sign of the Ravenous Goanna

At the sign of the Ravenous Goanna
I went to have a feed:
The thought was so exquisite
I was trembling at the knees.
They have Lamingtons in Batter,
And Licorice All-sorts Pie,
And Lamb's Fry served in Cold Custard
That you just have to try.
Vegemite, and Lipton's Tea
Dished up with Rabbit Stew,
And Two Fruits, lovely Two Fruits,
To thrill you through and through.
Tomato Sauce and Chocolate Frogs,
And Saunder's Malt Extract
(Just pity all the poor lost souls
Who've never tasted that!)
Dims Sims, Chooks, and Chico Rolls,
And good old boiled Galah;
Floaters and Vick's Vapo-Rub
For old men with catarrh.

Polly Waffles, Prickly Pear,
Johnny Cakes and Billy Tea;
Stewed Prune and Baked Bean Jaffles
-- Oh, Australian food for me!
There's Scotty's Wild Stuff Stew of course,
And Oysters from the Rocks,
And Wine, the nectar of the Grape,
Served from a cardboard box.
Peck's Fish Paste and Passion Fruit;
Teddy Bears with Robur Tea;
Pavlova, Chips and Choo-Choo Bars
—The Height of Luxury!
Yabbies, Jaffas, Saveloys,
Damper, Crays, Nardoo;
Jumbuk Pate for the pseudos,
Butter Menthols for the 'flu.
There's a dish for every taste and mood,
And they sing Australian songs.
So come to the Ravenous Goanna, friends,
And bring your friends along.

—Keith McKenry, 1970s.

1

The Aussie Way

The winds of a million years have made Australia into what she is today. There are few jagged peaks in the Outback. Instead, there are rocky outcrops worn round and smooth by the endless grinding of the elements. The reds of the Australian centre are matched in tone and intensity only by the scorched surface of Mars. It is a Timeless Land, as the great Australian novelist Eleanor Dark observed many years ago.

Australia's indigenous people are referred to as the timeless people, having inhabited Australia before time began. There are many aboriginal folk stories that preserve a sense of the sheer age of the land and her people, often referred to as the "dream time." Australia's unusual animals loom large in these stories, and well they should. Australia boasts animal species that are unique: Furred animals that lay eggs (the platypus); others that suckle their young in pouches (kangaroos); still others that get high on a naturally found drug (koalas); birds whose calls sound as raucous laughter (kookaburra); yet other birds that mimic all the sounds of the bush (the lyre bird).

Into this giant landscape stepped the English in the 1770s searching for somewhere to dump their convicts. The American Revolution made it impossible for the English to use America as its prison. There are many theories as to how the Australian national character—carefree (epitomized by the common saying, "she'll be right mate"), a bit abrasive and a most disarming, earthy, sense of humour—has evolved from that of criminals. Sir Robert Menzies (Australia's conservative prime minister for some 18 years ending in 1966) was always ready with an answer to those who made fun of Australia's convict ancestry. In a speech at the Jefferson Oration at Charlottesville, Virginia on the 4th of July, 1963, Sir Robert wryly noted, "...the records show that the great majority of persons convicted in England during the transportation era remained in England...."

The influence of the English on Australian lifestyles and customs is vast. We have them to thank for the national sport of cricket. Australia's unique sport, "Aussie Rules" football was, sort of, derived from Irish football. And we have the English to thank for our Irish heritage, since a large portion of convicts sent to Australia were Irish. Our rich array of folk songs and poetry are probably attributable to the oppression of convicts and settlers by the British and their lackeys in the early colonial period.

Most of all, though, the English have influenced Australian food, cooking and eating habits. Many of the oldest recipes in this book bear a strong similarity to English dishes. Fruit cake, steamed pudding, roast lamb, pasties and many others, are directly identifiable in English cuisine. But they have also become a central feature in traditional Australian cuisine, and are reasonably included as "Australian."

Traditional Australian Cooking

What is an authentic Australian dish? The answer to this difficult question is, any dish that Australians have taken to call their own. A dish that they eat as part of everyday life. Fish and Chips are English. But they are Australian too, and Australians have given them their special Australian "character," if one can refer to a French fry as having character. (Does one ever hear the claim that the English chip is really French?)

Older recipes form the major part of this book hoping to preserve the traditional Australian way of cooking that is fast disappearing, supplanted by exotic dishes from the far East and Europe. In the broad balance of things, this change is of course a good thing, because the range of dishes available to the Australian cook and diner is now just wonderful. Australian cities boast some of the best restaurants in the world. One can walk down any street in Australia's major cities (indeed, in country towns) and find restaurants from many different cultures from around the world. A separate chapter is included to reflect these recent changes, though it is hard to keep up with the changes of cuisine. There is also included a chapter on "Outback Cooking" that boasts "modern Australian" recipes, those that attempt to rediscover the indigenous Australian foods. One must admit that the changes are so rapid that by the time you get to read this book, it will most likely be out of date as far as modern Australian cuisine is concerned.

The traditional recipes in this book were gleaned from personal recipe files of friends and relatives. Sometimes these recipes have been a bit hard to decipher. Our parents and grandparents cooked most of their lives on a wood burning stove and oven. Their hand-written recipes mostly said, "warm," "moderate," or "hot" oven. The way they established whether the oven was ready, was to open the door and put in one's hand. It has been a challenge to translate these imprecise measurements into temperature settings. Most of these temperature settings have been translated into Celsius and Fahrenheit. and conversion charts can be found in the appendix.

Quantities are also difficult to translate because old Australian measurements, especially tablespoons, dessert spoons and liquid measures are quite different from the American. Most of these measurements have been converted into metric since this is the measure used in just about every country except the USA. Hopefully, these conversions are accurate, but just in case you should treat the measurements of the older traditional recipes as guides to be adjusted if you think things are not going quite right. In some recipes when there was some doubt, both types of measurement are provided. Conversion charts for Celsius to Fahrenheit can be found on the back of the book.

The Australian Outback and Bush Cooking

Four-fifths of Australia's almost 23 million inhabitants live in its five largest cities. This makes Australia one of the most sparsely populated yet most urbanized countries of the world! Many Australians have probably never seen a kangaroo in the wild (though if you know where to go, this is quite a simple thing to do), let alone actually try to live in the Outback. There are not really many authentic outback recipes, though there has been a renaissance in outback recipes of recent times, and in some popular restaurant chains, one even in America. These are modern, rather than traditional recipes. Most of these recipes use a few outback traditional ingredients (such as witchetty grubs) and produce a modern dish which largely masks the taste of the original ingredient. Many of the authentic outback dishes one can cook in America, although a few of the ingredients aren't available in the American forest, such as Tiger Snake. Substitutions can be made, though. And, if you really must have it, it is now possible to order and import such delicacies as witchetty grubs from Australia. A number of these "new traditional" recipes are included in Chapter 13.

"Strine" (the Aussie Language) and Cooking Traditions

Americans frequently ask whether Australians speak English. The answer is, "more or less." Of course, we do speak English, but with a heavy accent, with the voice directed somewhere down one's chest. If you say "newspiper" instead of "newspaper" you will have closely reproduced a typical Australian vowel sound. However, it is not so much the accents that make Australians difficult to understand, but the many unique expressions. There is a whole vocabulary, along with unusual usage of common words that can make conversation with an Australian something of an experience. An American friend once gave a speech to a large audience of Australian police, urging that people get off their fannies and work for a particular project. He was unaware that "fanny" did not mean "backside" in Australia as it does in the U.S., but rather refers to a very private female part! (Its usage has fallen away in recent years.)

There are also spelling differences and word usage between Australian English and that of USA. For the edification of American readers, the Australian usage has been retained. without which it would be difficult to describe eating and cooking traditions. Accordingly, we could say, "Bon Appetit" but the Australian saying is more earthy, in keeping with our convict ancestry:

"Two, Four, Six, Eight,
Bog in, don't wait!
--and enjoy your tucker (food)!

2

Pie 'n Sauce and other Aussie Classics

To be "fair dinkum" in the Australian language is to be "true blue." None the wiser? Both expressions mean absolutely pure and authentic. And that's what these foods are. They're pure Australian. It doesn't matter that they may have existed somewhere else (in Once-Great-Britain, for example) long before they became part of every Australian's life. What is important is that they are now totally unique to Australia. A spectator sport would be unthinkable without them. Just as a baseball game would be unthinkable without hot dogs.

Should you go to the cricket or footy (an Australian Rules football game) you will have many chances to buy a pie and sauce (and, if you're that way inclined, a beer to go with it). Meat pies are the take-out food in Australia. Some tasteless people, certainly not dinkum Aussies, have described Aussie meat pies as gravy encased in pieces of cardboard pastry. This may (only may) be true for mass produced pies, but it certainly is not true for those made at home.

Maisie's Pasties

Pronounced *parh-stees*, probably of Cornish origin, but definitely now Australian through and through. They are sometimes a different shape to that described in this recipe, which is the typical Cornish pasty shape. Along with fish and chips, hot dogs and pies, pasties are a favourite take-out food in Australia. Their aroma while cooking is nothing short of tantalizing. The unusual blend of vegetables and meat, encased in a delicious pastry makes them unique as take-out food—and probably the most nutritious. These days, vegetarian pasties are quite common. In fact, it's getting more and more difficult to buy a simple traditional pasty. The range of flavours and ingredients has increased immensely, particular with Asian and South Asian flavours and spices, not to mention very popular vegetarian pasties, usually heavily spiced, though. Unfortunately some Americans do not like pasties, and even Australians raised in the United States are not too thrilled about them. This seems to be  because of the turnip or rutabaga, which are not traditional favourites in Australia (though may be essential for various types of stews). One could make pasties without these vegetables, but then the pasties would lose their distinctive taste. Pasties are eaten with plenty of ketchup (tomato sauce to Australians). Some like them made with lots of pepper.

Filling

500 g. (1 lb.) lean ground beef
500 g. (1 lb.) potatoes
1 carrot
1 small turnip or rutabagas
2-3 medium onions
salt and pepper
Chop finely or mince all vegetables and add to the meat. Mix thoroughly, add salt and pepper.

Pastry

2 cups self-rising flour
1 cup margarine
⅓ cup water
1 pinch salt

1. Sift flour and salt, rub in margarine until mixture looks like bread crumbs. Mix in water gradually, stirring with a wooden spoon until

dough makes a stiff ball. If in doubt, it is better that the dough is a little moist than dry.
2. Turn on to a floured board and knead lightly. Cut into 12 pieces and knead into rounds. Roll out each round as thin as possible so that dough may be lifted and shaped without breaking.
3. Spoon mixture into centre of each piece of dough, then with a wet finger moisten the edges of each dough round.
4. Lift pastry up from sides, bringing it into the centre, and pinch together all across the top. Begin at centre and work towards the outside. Instead of pinching together at the top. Sometimes the mixture is placed on one side of the round, and the other half folded all the way over and pinched around the edge, making a kind of half circle shape (something like an apple turnover). Puff pastry is also sometimes used.
5. Place pasties on a greased cookie tray. Paint with egg or milk, then prick the tops with a fork.
6. Bake for ½ to ¾ hour at 175-200C (350-400F) until pastry is golden brown.

Pie 'n Sauce

Here is an all-time favourite recipe. It is for a 22 cm. pie pan. The pies one may buy in the store are usually a small one-serving size. The traditional shape was an oval, but this tradition disappeared many years ago, no doubt because the shape could not be adapted easily to mass production. Bought pies also have a pie crust on top and bottom, otherwise they would be difficult to eat in the hands. Even so, they are real hard to bite into without gravy shooting out over your shirt.

15 g. (½ oz.) butter
15 g. (½ oz.) onion (finely chopped)
¼ cup celery (finely chopped)
¼ cup carrots (finely chopped)
     250-375 g. (½ - ¾ lb.) ground beef
        or
        cubed steak
1 cup beef stock
1 recipe **Maisie's Pasties**

1. Roll beef in flour, or sprinkle 1 tablespoon of flour over ground beef.
2. Sauté beef in butter with onion, carrot and celery, until meat is brown and vegetables bright in colour.
3. Cover with beef stock, add salt and pepper to taste, and simmer covered until meat is tender.
4. Place in greased pie pan and top with pie crust).
5. Bake for 10-15 minutes at 220C (425F) or until pastry is golden brown.
6. Serve hot, always with plenty of ketchup (tomato sauce in Australian).

For **Steak and Kidney Pie**, the English ancestor of these pies, add 1 small chopped beef kidney to meat mixture. For **Party Pies,** line muffin tins with thin pastry, fill with pie filling, and cap. Try other variations: add a couple of spoons of frozen peas to the mixture when sautéing the meat and vegetables, and/or add 1 tablespoon of red wine. Or, try a teaspoon of port (yes, port). Can be frozen and reheated a week or two later.

Mom's Sausage Rolls

These little beauties appear in New Zealand, Scotland, England, Canada and even in Delaware, USA. While always delicious, the commercial variety never tastes the same as the real Australian, home made sausage roll, especially the ones Mum (Mom) used to make. The difference is in the pastry.

½ pound (250 g.) sausage meat
½ pound (250 g.) pastry
1 egg yolk
1 pastry recipe **Maisie's Pasties**

1. Roll out pastry into oblong shape and cut into 8 even pieces by cutting first straight down the centre of the pastry, then across 3 times.
2. Divide sausage meat into 8 pieces, roll each piece into a sausage shape and sprinkle all over with flour.
3. Place each sausage on the pastry, moisten the edges of pastry with water.
4. Fold over pastry so that it covers the sausage and meets on other side (see illustration). Press together with the back of a flat knife.
5. Beat yolk of egg and brush it on the rolls.
6. Bake in hot oven 190-205^C (400^F) for 20-30 minutes.

SECRET: Make sure your pastry is not too short (too dry), or it will be difficult to work over the sausage, and will also crumble when your eager guests try to get their mouths around these delicious morsels. In the USA there may be a problem with the sausage meat. In Australia this meat is usually finely ground beef, but sometimes pork is used. Pork sausage in the United States is fine, but be sure you buy extra lean, otherwise you may end up with sausage rolls floating around in a sea of fat. Ideally, the sausage should be finely ground as in pork sausage, but shaped lean ground beef, while not perfect, still provides a delicious roll. Link sausages or sausage meat will also do the job.

Pork Pies

250 g. (½ lb.) pork, minced (ground).
½ apple
½ onion
2 tablespoons flour
salt and pepper
½ pound pastry
½ cup water
Milk for top
1 pastry recipe, **Maisie's Pasties**

1. Chop apple and onion very fine.
2. Add flour, salt, pepper and water.
3. Simmer until apple and onion are soft.
4. Remove from heat and thoroughly mix into ground pork.
5. Line one well-greased muffin pan with thin pie crust.
6. Fill with mixture and cover tops with pastry.
7. Paint tops with milk, and prick with fork.
8. Bake in oven 190-205C (375-400F) for an hour.

About Pork Pies. Pork pies are definitely not a part of Australian cooking any more. They are certainly still very much a part of the English scene. One can find them along with Scotch eggs in just about every English pub. Not so in Australia. Old Australians consider pork to be very "sickly" only to be eaten on very special occasions. In fact, Australian pork does tend to be less lean than American, although the bacon is more lean. But, in deference to Australia's English heritage, this recipe is included. Actually, they pies are delicious. They probably were edged out of Australian pubs by beef pies and pasties which do go better with beer. Pork pies taste better with apple cider (effervescent and alcoholic, of course). The modern replacement of pork pies in Australian pubs and everywhere else is "pulled pork." No comment needed.

Egg and Bacon Pie

The chances are that, just as in the United States, *real* (that is, old) Australian men don't eat *quiche*, but you can be sure that they do eat egg and bacon pie which is very similar, if not better than *quiche*. Try it, and decide for yourself.

4-5 large eggs
½ cup milk
2 tablespoons parsley
1 small onion (finely chopped)
¼ cup grated cheese
½ cup chopped bacon (lean is best)
1 pastry recipe **Maisie's Pasties**

1. Roll out pastry thinly and line a 22.5 cm. pie pan.
2. Place 3 eggs, cheese, onions, milk and salt and pepper in pan and beat with a fork until blended well.
3. Heat over slow flame, like cooking scrambled eggs. Stir continually. When mixture has consistency of lightly scrambled eggs mix in parsley.
4. Pour into pie pan and cover with pieces of bacon and break open 1 or 2 eggs to bake on top.
5. Bake at 175 °C (350F) for 30 minutes.

Rupanyup Rissoles

These are interesting hybrids, half hamburger and half croquette. Traditional Aussie moms used to make rissoles often, using minced up or diced leftover meat, whether lamb, veal or beef.

Meat patties

125 g. (4 oz.) ground beef
½ teaspoon basil
4 tablespoons bread
2 tablespoons parsley (finely chopped)
bread crumbs
1 egg
⅓ cup beef bouillon

1. Lightly brown ground beef over high heat.
2. Add remaining ingredients, lower heat and stir until mixture is quite thick.
3. Add bread crumbs or bouillon until correct thickness is obtained. Remove from pan and set aside to cool.

Coating

1 egg
½ cup bread crumbs
4 tablespoons flour
2 tablespoons parsley
pepper and salt (finely chopped)

1. Using a tablespoon, form mixture into patties, and roll in flour, salt and pepper. Beat egg and brush over rissole, then roll on bread crumbs, pushing crumbs into surface with a knife.
2. Heat cooking oil, and when hot, place rissoles in pan and fry each side until golden brown. When cooked, drain on paper.
3. Serve garnished with parsley, and with brown gravy. Ketchup or a packet of brown gravy is also fine. Gravox is the Aussie favourite.

Toad-In-The-Hole

This meat and batter dish is popular for breakfast, lunch or dinner

½ cup self-rising flour
1 egg
250 g.. (8 oz.) sausage meat or sausages
30 g. (1 oz.) margarine
¾ cup milk
salt

1. Sift flour, add melted margarine and stir into flour, gradually adding milk (make tepid). Beat well, fold in beaten egg just before using.
2. Shape sausage meat into sausage shapes. Grease baking pan and place in a hot oven (205 C, 400F) until very hot.
3. Pour in the batter, drop in the sausages so that they lie in one direction.
4. Bake for 35 minutes. Best served with thick brown gravy, or ketchup.

About sausage meat: You will have to experiment with sausage meat. If you decide to use pork sausage, ask your butcher for pork sausage that is very lean, otherwise you may have underground rivers of fat, rather than toads in the hole. If you would rather play it safe, the older, though less common Australian version of this dish-with-the-strange-name was made with pieces of good quality steak or cubed lamb. In America extra lean ground beef works well. This dish is also essentially English in origin. The Australian version is far better, though, because it uses snags (the long thin ones) as the sausage meat. Sausage links (American) could be substituted. So could hot dogs.

3
Sandwiches and Scones

American friends who have visited Australia have been shocked at what they rather uncharitably termed "the little things Australians call sandwiches." Things have changed a lot, though. The size of Aussie sandwiches (and generally portions served in restaurants) is rapidly catching up to the American giants. It is customary for an American sandwich to contain a quarter pound (125 g..) of "cold cuts" (cold cooked meat) in a sandwich served in a typical deli in the American North East.

There are basically two kinds of sandwiches in Australia: (1) those that are cut by thousands of mums (and maybe now dads) every day for school and work lunches, and (2) those prepared for afternoon teas. There is not a great deal of difference between the two, as far as fillings go, but they are both vastly different from an American sandwich. Here's why.

Australian sandwiches are almost always cut from a small sized sandwich loaf (the most common are white and "wholemeal" though these days there is about as big a variety of bread as in America). Without exception, the bread for every sandwich is cut thinner than in America, in fact the thinner the better. In addition, each slice of bread is spread with a thin layer of butter or margarine. Again, this is without exception, no matter the filling—even peanut butter.

If one is preparing sandwiches for an afternoon tea or a kid's birthday party (yes, believe it or not, there are sandwiches that are quite acceptable to kids for a birthday party—read on!) the practice is to cut off all the crusts, making the overall size of the bread slice even smaller. Then the sandwiches are cut diagonally so that small dainty triangles are produced. Squares and rectangles are also acceptable, but they are the exception.

Now for the "meagre fillings." It is largely because of the butter in the sandwiches that there is less filling. If one buys a roast beef sandwich in Australia one may receive two or three thin slices, four at the most in the sandwich. It is not quantity that is important, but a particular taste. One should add that meats tend to be much more cooked in Australia than the United States. Anyway it is probably the acquired taste of butter in the sandwich that satisfies the Australian appetite. If there were any more filling the sandwich would be too sickly.

The more usual sandwich lunch would be "two rounds of sandwiches" (although the sandwiches are square, not round). This means 4 slices of bread made into two sandwiches, each sandwich possibly with a different filling, but a filling no more than ¼ inch thick. In a sandwich shop, packets of mixed sandwiches are common. Again, these will have very meagre fillings, by American standards, but will have three or four different fillings, and will usually contain 2 rounds of sandwiches (i.e. 4 slices of bread).

Today, one may observe the steady incursion of wraps, pitas, bargettes, focaccias, Turkish, Indian, Middle Eastern and many other breads into the Aussie sandwich realm. The days of the Aussie sandwich may be over. Though they do feature in high class restaurants that serve posh afternoon teas, trying to be as English as possible.

And then there are the scones. Scones have infiltrated pretty much every coffee shop in America and international airports. Unfortunately, they have no resemblance to the Aussie scone, as we will in detail shortly. Suffice it to say that the scone you get in a Starbucks (no matter what country) is OK as far as it goes, but it just isn't like a real scone (Aussie that is). More on this later.

Vegemite Sandwich

For special occasions, which include parties, special teas, or for someone who is feeling down (Vegemite is the chicken soup of Aussie mums) these sandwiches are often served open style. The bread should be as fresh as possible and sliced thinly.

1. Spread bread lightly with butter or margarine. Place a small amount of Vegemite on the tip of a knife and spread very thinly over bread and butter.
2. Cut into dainty shapes. Butter and Vegemite may also be spread on any type of cracker. And it's great on toast (buttered of course).

Be warned! Not many Americans like this stuff. It's a taste that is carefully cultivated among Australian kids virtually from birth. It also tastes very salty, although now there is a version that is low salt. It says on the Vegemite jar label that this dark, iodine coloured substance is a vegetable yeast extract. Folklore has it that many years ago, a bright young chemist developed it from the enormous amounts of by-products from beer manufacture. Perhaps you have not heard, but Australians are devoted beer drinkers.

About Vegemite. "Vegemite" is a trademark of Kraft Foods (believe it or not!). It may be found occasionally in American gourmet food stores, although its (lesser) counterpart, Marmite (a beef extract a bit like bouillon paste) is more common, also, English, not Australian.

Tomato Sandwich

Slice bread (the freshest possible—there's nothing worse than tomato sandwiches on one day old bread) as thinly as possible. Spread each slice with butter or margarine. Select a firm ripe tomato and slice very thinly. Place one layer of tomato on bread, sprinkle with salt and pepper to taste, close sandwich, cut into triangles.

No, nothing has been left out. In America if you ask for a grilled tomato sandwich at a local cafeteria, you will get the response, "you mean cheese and tomato?" Sometimes it's easier to ask for a BLT (the staple American sandwich of bacon, lettuce and tomato) without lettuce, bacon, or mayo but with a little butter! It's an expensive way to buy it, but sometimes it's the only way one can convince the waitress (or the chef) to prepare a sandwich with just tomato!

In the golden years of the Aussie sandwich, tomato sandwiches were virtually the staple Australian food (excluding beer, that is). Today, this tradition may be transitioning towards mixing other fillings with the tomato, the most popular being ham. In fact, in a wonderful example of reverse cultural incursion, Aussie restaurants feature a BLAT (Bacon, Lettuce, Avocado and Tomato). And now, smashed avocado has become an international hit on breakfast and brunch menus. An Aussie first!

Other Sandwich Fillings

Try these fillings in your small, thin sandwiches. Remember to butter the bread. When making these sandwiches at home, Aussies would probably not mix the fillings. Sandwich shops these days offer these and many other fillings, and customers may commonly request many different combinations of fillings. Actually, one doubts that any sandwich shops exist these days. They have been replaced by "sub" shops.

diced asparagus (a Queensland favourite in season).
processed cheese and diced celery
tomato and cucumber
cucumber
sardines
vegemite and cheese
corned beef and pickles
apples and raisins
cheese and raisins
ham and mustard
diced boiled eggs and lettuce
German sausage* and ketchup ("tomato sauce" in Australia.)
cold leftover spaghetti
cold baked beans
salmon

*German sausage is the Australian equivalent to Bologny sausage in America. The taste is a little more spiced, but the consistency of the sausage is very similar. A few of these fillings may seem a little "yucky" to you, especially the cold spaghetti. But note that these sandwiches have very little filling, half a centimetre at the most. You'll be surprised how good they taste.

Fairy Bread

Spread fresh slices of both brown and white bread lightly with butter. Top with a generous amount of rainbow sprinkles (called "hundreds and thousands" in Australia), cut into dainty sizes. Do not try to spread after you have put on the sprinkles, or the colours will run into the butter. Chocolate sprinkles are also enjoyed, although the expression "hundreds and thousands" is a term most often associated with very special occasions like kids' birthday parties.

Potted Meat Sandwich

This is a very, very old recipe that our grandmothers used to make. I doubt that mothers (or fathers) of today either have the time or make the time to cook this delicacy of old.

500 g.. (1 lb.) lean steak
4 tablespoons Worcestershire sauce
125 g.. (4 oz.) butter
¾ teaspoon cayenne pepper
½ teaspoon mace
½ teaspoon ground nutmeg
salt to taste

1. Trim fat off meat, cut into small squares.
2. Add all ingredients and steam in basin for 4 hours.
3. Mince twice and mix into own gravy. Do not add water.
4. Place in bowl, cover, and refrigerate.
5. When set, may be used as cold meat sliced for salads. Or, may be used as a spread for sandwiches.

Old Australian menus rarely included pâté, as known in French cuisine. However, the wide variety of potted meats available in Australia more than made up for this gap. An exception is a product called Peck's Paste, a perennial favourite for a couple of generations. These pastes are sold in the supermarket, and there are many varieties, including fish paste, chicken, ham and other combinations. Needless to say, if used for sandwiches, the bread is always buttered, and only a thin spread of these pastes is applied.

Hamburger with the Works

Hamburgers are about as American as one can get, though the name obviously is not American. Since the fast food chains moved into Australia, the (almost) indigenous Australian hamburger got a fright, then blossomed. An American friend who went on a business trip to Sydney some years ago would no doubt applaud this Darwinian fate of the Aussieburger. This is because he thinks that they are the wrong colour! (See below.)

500 g. (1 lb.) lean ground beef
1 onion finely chopped
1 small carrot grated
1 small can beets (beetroot)
1 thick slice of Aussie cheddar.
1 egg
lettuce, ketchup, tomato, fried egg
hard rolls

1. Lightly sauté onion and carrot, allow to cool.
2. In large bowl, thoroughly mix ground beef ("mincemeat" in Australia), lightly beaten egg, onion and carrot.
3. Press into patties and broil or fry according to taste.
4. Insert along with all ingredients above, into a hard roll.

While this recipe is not especially different from any recipe one would find in an American cookbook, there is one ingredient sneaked into the burger that sets it apart, and ruins its colour—beets. In Australia, beet root (as beets are called) rears its ugly, velvety-red head in many unexpected places. When our American friend ordered an Aussieburger, and replied that, yes, he would have it with "the works," liberal amounts of beet root were inserted. Unlike other hamburger ingredients, such as lettuce or tomato, beet root won't keep to itself. It seeps everywhere, and colours most of the hamburger purple!. Australians not only enjoy beets in their hamburgers, they even eat beetroot sandwiches, on buttered bread of course!

Salad Rolls

Years ago (decades), on the few occasions when we kids bought their lunch at school, they would look forward to a salad roll (for one of us, without beet root, thank you!). These rolls are simple to make, and today, because they have nothing but vegetables in them might be seen as the food of vegetarians. Of course, there is nothing to stop one from adding one's favourite cold cuts. Chicken or ham are a popular addition to this vegetarian fare. Not to mention butter (non-dairy if you like).

beets (beetroot)
fresh crisp lettuce
thinly sliced firm tomato
grated carrot
thinly sliced cucumber
well chopped onion
thin slice of orange

These ingredients should be placed in hard crisp rolls that have been lavishly spread with butter or margarine. One may have difficulty finding rolls that are similar to those used in Australia. The closest are called at an Italian American bakery, "crispy torpedoes." Add salt and pepper to taste. Salad dressing would not normally be added—the butter serves this purpose. Many of the Australian hard crispy rolls are round, not submarine shaped. Except for the shape, one can see that these salad rolls are a close cousin to the popular American submarine. These days crispy rolls are hard to come by. They have gone the way of the American Hamburger roll, though, thankfully, not the whole way. They may be found in boutique or country bakeries. And one final indication of cultural degradation: mayonnaise has seeped its way into Aussie subs and hamburgers alike.

Toasties

Grilled Cheese

thick slices of bread
slices of processed cheese
butter

Methods

1. **Broiled open sandwich.** Place slices of bread under broiler and toast one side only.
2. Remove, spread untoasted side lightly with butter, cover with one or two (no more!) slices of cheese.
3. Return to broiler and toast until cheese melts or browns on top. Cut into squares, serve immediately.

1. **Grilled sandwich.** Make a regular cheers sandwich, buttering both sides of the bread.
2. Place on a hot plate to grill (that is brown on one side as in grilling pancakes),
3. When one side is done, flip and grill the other side.

One should also distinguish the Australian toasted sandwich from the sandwich that one might order in America, by saying something like, "BLT on whole wheat toast, please." In America, they usually toast the bread separately, then make the sandwich. In Australia, they make the sandwich, then toast the whole thing. Of course, they do not put the whole sandwich in a pop-up toaster. That doesn't work too well. Rather, the whole sandwich is placed on the hot plate—or the griller that squeezes the sandwich between two heated surfaces so that both sides are grilled at the same time. All sandwiches may from time to time be treated in this way, but the out-and-out favourites are cheese, tomato and ham. We have even known some to eat toasted peanut butter sandwiches. Don't forget to butter the bread!

Dad's Scones

"Scone" rhymes with "con" (as in convict) in Australian. It should be the same in American, although to an Australian ear, Americans usually say "scone" more like "cone." A scone is almost the same as an American soda biscuit. Or it used to be. Scones have become very popular in the USA, especially in coffee shops (yes, Starbucks), but these, while often quite tasty, do not resemble Aussie scones at all. They are too "short" or crumbly, and too dry. For reasons difficult to understand, in Australia scones are widely considered the most elementary of cooking skills. But they are very difficult to cook well and there is much folklore about how to make scones turn out light and fluffy.

3 cups self-rising flour
90 g. (3 oz.) margarine
1 teaspoon white vinegar
1 pint milk

1. Mix vinegar with milk to curdle.
2. Sift flour, rub in margarine until mixture is like oatmeal.
3. Add milk gradually and work with wooden spoon. Work dough until it becomes sloppy and sticks to the fingers.
4. Knead dough until it is no longer sticky on the outside.
5. Pat out to about 1 inch thick, and cut with a glass dipped in flour or a round cookie cutter.
6. Preheat oven to 230C (450F)
7. Grease cookie tray, and place in oven to warm a little.
8. Arrange the scones on the tray so they almost touch.
9. Paint tops with melted butter or milk.
10. Place on top rung of oven, cook 8-10 minutes at 230$^{C.}$

Make sure your oven is very hot. Depending on your oven, you might even need to make it a little hotter than 230C.
Do not allow to cool on tray. Immediately remove and place in a wicker type basket, wrapped lightly in a thin cloth.
Serve warm if possible. Irresistible with jam and cream.

Elsie's Scones

1 cup self-rising flour
1 cup whole wheat flour
90 (3 oz.) g. butter
1 teaspoon sugar water

1. Sift flour and sugar into basin and rub butter into mixture until it has the consistency of oatmeal.
2. Add water and mix until a soft dough is obtained.
3. Tip out onto board and knead well.
4. Roll out to about 1 inch thick, cut into circles.
5. Place on greased cookie tray, bake 10 minutes in hot oven (205C, 400F).
6. Wrap loosely in light cloth to cool. Serve warm if possible.

Australians like scones just with plain butter when served hot. If served cool, they are the number one item for an afternoon tea. In this case, serve in wicker basket and allow guests to open the cloth to retrieve a scone. Provide whipped cream and a range of jellies and preserves for toppings, if guests are seated at table. Otherwise break the scones in half and add toppings. Don't butter if you top with whipped cream and preserves.

Variations: Add 60 g. of currants to the above mixture for delicious fruit scones. Alternatively, substitute for the sugar, 2-3 ounces of parmesan cheese for tangy cheese scones.

Lemonade Scones. These are truly a great scone and are a terrific way to introduce very willing kids to cooking.

3 cups self-rising flour
1 cup fresh full cream
1 cup lemonade (in America, "11-up.")

1. Pre-heat oven to 200^C.
2. Mix flour, cream and lemonade to form a soft dough.
3. Turn and knead lightly until combined.
4. Press the dough to a thickness of about 2 cm.
5. Use a 6 cm round cutter to cut out scones,
6. place on baking tray and brush the tops with some milk.
7. Bake for 10-15 minutes until lightly browned.

Aussie Snacks

Cheese and Bacon Squares

1 sliced sandwich loaf
1 cup grated cheese
250 g. (8 oz.) lean bacon
1 egg
butter

1. Trim crusts from bread slices, spread lightly with butter and cut into squares.
2. Mix cheese and egg well, then spoon on to bread.
3. Preheat oven to 190.
4. place squares on cookie tray, and bake until golden brown.

These are wonderful for breakfast ("brekkie" to Australians) and make impressive savories. Try freezing them and heat in a toaster oven for supper (that is, a bed time snack.)

Maisie's Cheese Straws
6 tablespoons butter
12 tablespoons self-rising flour
12 tablespoons extra sharp cheese
sprinkle cayenne pepper
desiccated (flaked) coconut

1. Knead butter, flour, cheese and pepper together to make a pastry.
2. Roll thinly on a pastry sheet sprinkled with coconut.
3. Cut into straws and roll in more coconut.
4. Bake on a tray in a moderate oven for about 15 minutes. Take care not to burn the coconut.
5. Cool on a wire rack and keep in an air tight tin or container.

Savory, crisp and delicious with a pre-dinner drink. Serves 8 or more, depending on thickness.

4

Prawns, Snags and other Barbie Delights

The Australian Barbecue (Barbie) has become a great institution. It is by far the most popular way of cooking, especially when entertaining. The temperate climate makes it possible to spend a lot of time out of doors, which is where Australians like to be.

Get in lots of steak, lamb chops (the little ones with the curly tails that cost a fortune in the United States, but are relatively cheap in Australia), snags (sausages), a gas barbecue and plenty of beer, and you're set to entertain any number of easily satisfied guests.

Roasts are also very common in Australia, and are these days often cooked on the Barbie. In the old days, of course, the roast was cooked every Sunday. Mum would put the roast in the oven, and it would be left to cook while all went to church. Whatever the roast, it would be very well done. By and large, older Australians, tend to eat meat well done.

About Aussie Barbies. Every person who claims to be a "true blue" Aussie (authentic Aussie) MUST have a barbie. These come in many different varieties, but probably the most popular are gas grills, the same as those found in the United States. Most public parks and recreational areas provide barbies for local use. These may be either gas or electric, and may be coin operated, and very often are free. Barbecues that rely on fires (charcoal, and even gas) are often not available because they are considered a fire risk in times of high fire danger.

Queensland Grill

750 g. (1¼ lb.) choice steak cut into 4 slices*
2 small bananas
4 slices fresh pineapple
½ cup medium dry sherry
freshly ground pepper

*Trying to match American steaks to Australian steaks is very difficult. Australian butchers cut their meat differently from American. A large London Broil, as thick a piece of steak as possible, comes very close to the Australian steak in this and other recipes. One can then cut the broil into slices of the thickness for the particular recipe.

1. Cut a pocket in each piece of steak and insert sliced banana.
2. Pour a teaspoon of sherry in each, and close with a toothpick.
3. Sprinkle with pepper and pour remaining sherry over top and allow to stand at least 4 hours.
4. Place steak on grill and cook to desired doneness. Just before serving place pineapple slices on top and heat briefly. Remove toothpicks and top with parsley butter.

Parsley Butter
4 tablespoons butter
1 tablespoon chopped fresh parsley

Beat butter and parsley, with a pinch of salt and pepper, into a smooth paste.

About Queensland: This North Eastern state was named by Queen Victoria in 1859, and is often called the "Sunshine State."

Pocket Steak Melbourne

500 g. (1 lb.) choice steak (2 pieces)
2 tablespoons onion, finely chopped
1 cup sliced mushrooms
60 g. (2 oz.) butter
salt and pepper
garlic butter

1. Trim any excess fat from steak, and cut a pocket in each piece.
2. Melt butter and sauté onion and mushrooms until onion is transparent.
3. Season with salt and pepper, then fill each pocket with mixture, sealing with toothpick.
4. Brush steak with garlic butter, then salt and pepper, place steak on grill.
5. Quickly turn to other side and repeat procedure. Cook to desired doneness.

Garlic Butter
Crush 1 clove of garlic, add salt and cayenne pepper and beat into 60 g. of butter until creamy.

About Melbourne: The second largest city in Australia, probably the culinary capital of Australia.

Steak and Onions

No country could lay claim to this dish as uniquely its own. Australia has its own version of this popular way to fix steak.

750 g. (312 oz.) choice steak
⅓ cup flour
1½ cups bread crumbs
2 eggs, beaten
90 g. (3 oz.) butter
3 onions, sliced
2 tablespoons milk
salt and pepper

1. Choose a thick London Broil and cut it into thin slices.
2. Dip each slice in flour, beaten eggs and milk, then in bread crumbs. Coat each side well.
3. Melt butter and lay steak on hot plate, or on grill covered with aluminium foil.
4. On side or next to steak, sauté onions until golden brown.
5. Season with salt and pepper.
6. Cook steak to desired doneness, then serve smothered with onions.

Variation: Cook your steak on a barbecue using a **beer sauce**. In a beer drinking country like Australia, what better sauce to baste your barbecue!

1 ½ cups tomato purée
1 can (375 ml) beer
6 tablespoons Worcestershire sauce
¼ cup cider vinegar
1 teaspoon paprika
1 teaspoon salt
½ teaspoon pepper

Combine all ingredients and heat to a simmer. Brush over meat every 5 minutes until meat has cooked.

More variations. If you are cooking lighter meats such as pork chops or chicken, use an ale or light beer. If red meats are to be basted, use a dark beer, or to avoid sweetness, use imported Guinness Stout. To baste lamb, substitute rosemary for the paprika, and use a light beer.

Steak Dianne

2 tablespoons Worcestershire sauce
1 clove garlic (finely chopped)
salt and pepper
60 g. (2 oz.) butter
¼ cup chopped parsley
choice steak

1. Using meat mallet, pound steak until about 1 inch (3 cm) thick.
2. Rub in salt and pepper.
3. Bring butter to a sizzle, toss in meat and cook in hot pan 1 minute or less on each side.
4. Turn back to first side, sprinkle with half the garlic and parsley and cook for 1 minute or less, then do same on other side.
5. Add Worcestershire sauce and cook 1 minute more. Lift steak on to serving dish, cover with sauce from pan.

Old Australians like this dish served with a crisp salad on the same plate. Steak Dianne is a universal favourite. One can hardly claim that it is an especially Australian dish. Yet, when one considers the early history of Australian foods—largely English in origin, which was to stick to plain and simple food, without any strong herbs or spices—Steak Dianne holds a special place. It was among the first of the more "spiced" or fancy dishes found acceptable by older Australians.

Aussie Mixed Grill

Because of the unavailability in the United States of one of the ingredients of this dish (snags), one can only approximate the Australian version of a mixed grill. The required ingredients are:

choice steak
bacon
large mushrooms
snags (sausages)
loin lamb chops
butter
tomatoes, halved

1. Grill each item to the desired doneness.
2. While meat is cooking, grill bacon until crisp, and sauté mushroom in butter.
3. When meat is almost cooked, place tomato halves on burner hotplate and cook till sizzling.
4. Turn out on to plates pre-warmed, placing bacon over lamb chop, and mushroom over steak. Australians like this dish with French fries (chips to Aussies).

Among certain hard working Aussies individuals who like a big brekkie, (breakfast) a mixed grill may find special attraction.

Unfortunately, replicating this recipe for Americans is hard because there is no equivalent in America to snags. The closest are sausage links, but these are usually way too spicy, the wrong shape, and don't have enough bread in them. Australian sausages come in two sizes. Short and fat (Usually pork sausages) and long and thin (slightly longer than a regular hot dog). Expatriate Aussies dream about them at least once a week. The traditional Aussie snag, though, is rapidly being transformed into all kinds of flavours, imported from Asia, South Asia, South East Asia and various Pacific Islands, not to mention Italy and other European sausage lovers.

Barbie Roast Leg of Lamb

1 leg of lamb (2 kg., 5-6 lb.)
4 large potatoes peeled, cut in large chunks
4 whole medium onions peeled
2 large carrots cut in large chunks
2 large parsnips cut in large chunks
250 g. (½ lb.) pumpkin cut in large chunks
250 g. (½ lb.) fresh peas
mint sauce

1. Start barbie on low heat, cover down.
2. Depending on the type of lamb, you may need to paint the lamb with oil. Australian lamb usually does not require it.
3. Allow 25 minutes per pound of meat. Check and turn every 15-20 minutes.
4. Parboil potatoes, onions, carrots, parsnips, pumpkin and add to hot plate of barbie about 1 hour before serving.
5. Lightly boil peas.
6. Remove roast from barbie.
7. Carve thin slices of lamb, place on preheated plates.
8. Carefully arrange selection of barbie-roasted vegetables on each person's plate. Add spoonful of peas to each serving.
9. Bring each plate to guests seated at dining table.
10. Pass around rich brown gravy and mint sauce.

Mint Sauce
2 tablespoons fresh mint, finely chopped
¼ cup boiling water
½ cup white wine vinegar
2 tsp caster sugar
Wash and dry the mint; finely chop. Pour over boiling water, add sugar and stir until dissolved. Add vinegar, stir. Serve in small jug with teaspoon.

About the Australian Roast. The traditional way of serving the roast was to prepare each individual diner's plate in advance, with each prepared plate brought to the diner at the table, as in a restaurant. In modern times, it is more likely that the various dishes would be passed around for each to take his or her portion, as is the common practice in America.

Zucchini Burgers

500 g. (1 lb.) lean ground beef (mince meat)
2-3 zucchini, grated
1 small onion, grated
1 teaspoon soy sauce
1 teaspoon grated green ginger
1 egg yolk
hamburger buns
lettuce, tomato and onion

Combine all ingredients, except buns and salad. Shape into six patties. Barbecue or pan fry until done to your liking. Serve on toasted buns with salad. Lovely moist burger. Great for the barbecue. Makes 6 burgers.

Seafood Skewers (Kabobs) with Lime Dill Butter

1 kg. (2 lb.) king shrimp
500 g. (1 lb.) scallops
lime wedges – optional

2 egg yolks
1 teaspoon grated lime rind
2 tablespoons lime juice
125 g. (4 oz.) butter
2 tablespoons chopped dill.

1. Peel and devein shrimp, leaving tail intact.
2. Thread shrimp, scallops and lime wedges into skewers.
3. Brush with sesame oil and BBQ on a hot plate. Cook quickly and serve with dill butter.

Lime dill butter

1. Place egg yolks, rind and juice in a basin over hot water whisk 1 minute.
2. Chop butter into small pieces and whisk into the egg mixture.
3. When sauce thickens remove from heat, stir in dill and cool.
4. May be made 2 days ahead. Bring to room temperature before using.

Serves 6.

Chilli Prawns (Shrimp) and Scallops

1 kg. (2 lb.) green king prawns
500 g. (1 lb.) scallops
⅓ cup oil
3 tablespoons honey
3 tablespoon chili sauce
2 tablespoons lemon juice
2 shallots chopped
¼ teaspoon five spice powder

1. Shell prawns leaving tails intact, remove vein.
2. Combine marinade ingredients in a bowl, mix well.
3. Mix prawns and scallops in marinade, leave 1 to 2 hours.
4. Thread scallops onto skewers in the curl of the prawn.
5. Barbecue quickly. Brush with marinade during cooking.
6. Cook 2 to 5 minutes max. Serves 6.

Noel's BBQ Bugs Risque

Fresh bugs, 4 halves per serve
60 g.. butter
Rind and juice of 1 lemon

1. 1 teaspoon chopped fresh ginger
2. 1 tablespoon chopped coriander
3. Cut bugs in half long ways.
4. Devein and drain.
5. Make herb butter by combining butter, ginger, lemon juice and rind. Beat well.
6. Add finely chopped coriander. Put into piping bag and pipe onto bug meat. Refrigerate for 30 minutes.
7. Place bugs on grill, butter side up. Cook about 10 minutes, depending on the size of the bug.

About Bugs. These strange creatures are a crustacean of ancient origin, similar to lobster in that all the meat is in the tail. The bug does not have any claws. In fact it looks a bit like a lobster without the claws. They are found in many of the bays along the eastern coast of Australia and are as expensive as lobsters (crayfish in Australia).

5

Fish, Chook and Rabbit

Australia has an enormous coastline because it is both a continent and an island. One would expect a nation of fishermen and fish eaters. This is not the case. Instead, Australia has been, until very recently, a nation of sheep, cattle and wheat farmers. And the bulk of the population in the cities has eaten the foods they produced.

In the last two decades of the 20th century, Australia became a frontier land all over again. New mining towns opening up in outback regions, and industrial suburbs cropped up everywhere. Fish consumption has not increased particularly, though that perennial favourite, fish and chips has steadfastly withstood the onslaught of American fast food chains. More chooks (chickens) are eaten, though, because mass farming and marketing of chickens has grown. Although there are many rural homes with chooks in their back yards, very few of these families would kill their own chooks for the table. It's easier to buy them, after all. Back yard chooks are kept mainly for their eggs. In the city, though, it's against the law to keep chooks in your back yard. So you have to make do with the warbling of magpies to wake you in the morning.

Rabbit was common up to the first half of the 20th century. It is now mostly available in gourmet restaurants or food stores. The reasons for the demise of rabbit as a common Australian food are many, some of which it is best not to know about. The Australian government has sponsored many different attempts to reduce the rabbit population. Not so many people catch their own rabbits any more.

But in the 21st century rabbits are making a comeback. The attempts to eradicate them have been a bit of a failure, and they are beginning to appear in restaurant menus once again. Some individuals have begun to farm rabbits for sale to butcher shops and anyone else who would buy them. It's likely that rabbits became less popular in the last decades of the 20th century because chicken became more widely available and affordable. Years ago grown-ups jokied about whether a dish, presented as chicken, really was chicken, and not rabbit in disguise. Rabbit was much cheaper and more widely available in the old days.

Fish and Chips are represented as an English invention, which one must grudgingly admit. However, just as spaghetti has been re-invented by a number of cultures (China, Italy and America to name but a few), so have fish and chips or French fries. The fact is that French fries taste different everywhere, even in fast food chain restaurants. There are important reasons for this, and important eating traditions that go along with these different types of French fries.

In Australia there are shops devoted entirely and only to selling fish and chips. While some of these shops might provide seating, it is generally expected that you will take your fish and chips out. There are probably no fish and chip shops in Australia that are either owned or run by Pommies (i.e. English). They are invariably owned by what used to be called in the 1950s "new Australians," —Australia's older immigrants, generally of Mediterranean origin.

Fish and Chips

250 g. (½ lb.) fish fillets*
½ cup of flour
1 pinch salt
1 teaspoon cooking oil
2 eggs
1¼ cups warm water
potatoes peeled and diced
cooking oil for chips
cooking oil for fish fry

1. Sift flour and salt together and make into a mound.
2. Make a hole in centre and pour oil in, then stir with a wooden spoon, adding water slowly.
3. Mix until a smooth paste is obtained.
4. Separate whites from eggs and beat to a stiff froth, fold lightly into flour mixture.
5. Wipe fish fillets dry with paper towel, dip in flour, then into batter. Heat oil in pan, add fish and cook briskly until golden brown.
6. Chips: Dice potatoes into desired shapes. Wipe off excess moisture with paper towel, fry in hot oil.

Serve fish and chips with a slice of lemon, salt, and a salad (on same plate) of lettuce and tomato. Vinegar is popular for the fish, especially among pommies. Never, repeat, never pour ketchup on your chips. This is an American influence strongly resisted by true-blue Aussies! Well, this used to be the case. The fact is that today it's OK to dip your chips in whatever concoction one likes. You can even get "batter fried chips" at many pubs and restaurants.

About fish fillets. The favourite fish for fish and chips varies depending on the region in Australia. In Southern Victoria, whiting is the clear favourite, though now very expensive. More common is a fish called "flathead," bountiful in the bays and coastal inlets of Australia. In America, frozen whiting is probably the best fish to use, although it does not have the rich taste of Australian whiting.

Grilled Flounder

Select a large, whole flounder. Fresh flounder can be identified by bright prominent eyes, firm flesh and an agreeable smell. If in doubt, don't buy it. Do not use this recipe for flounder fillets.

1. Wash flounder well, remove head if desired. It is unnecessary to skin this fish. The flounder is a flat fish with both eyes on one side of its body.
2. Turn over so that the underside (usually white in colour) faces up and paint liberally with parsley butter.
3. Place on grill and cook for 5 minutes or until browning occurs.
4. Remove, turn over carefully so that cooked flesh does not break, and repeat process for top side (usually dark in colour). Cook until brown.
5. Serve on a large plate with chips (French fries), garnished with crisp salad of lettuce and tomato, and slice of lemon.

How to Eat it. Grilled whole flounder is a popular pub restaurant item. Australians like them so that they cover almost an entire oval shaped plate. A simple trick will make your eating of the flounder more enjoyable. Begin by eating first one side, then turn the flounder completely over and eat the other side. Taking a little more care with the fin area, this makes the flounder an easy fish to eat without too much worry about loose bones. Whole flounder tastes completely different from the flounder fillets one finds in America. The meat is richer in flavour, and the texture is more flaky, less stringy.

How to catch. Take a long pole and attach a small light on the end, waterproof of course. Make or buy a spear, three pronged, about 5 feet long. Flounder are attracted to the light (the dark early morning hours are the favourite times to fish) and when they come up close can be speared. Alas, pollution and over fishing has eliminated the possibility of doing this anymore. And you will need a licence to fish.

Crayfish Salad

a large crayfish (steamed)
Sydney Rock Oysters
cooked medium shrimp
deep fried Tasmanian scallops (cold)
fresh garden vegetables for salad

1. Break open the crayfish by slicing down the middle.
2. Scoop out meat.
3. On a very large salad plate, arrange crisp lettuce leaves and place morsels of crayfish in each leaf.
4. Arrange legs and shell for decorative appearance, perhaps surround or fill with scallops, and or shrimp.
5. Place Sydney rock oysters (raw and on the shell) with half slice of lemon around plate.
6. Add firm slices of tomato, celery sticks, orange slices and carrot sticks to plate.
7. Provide a small jar of cocktail sauce and small jar of paste from head of the crayfish (called "mustard" because it looks like mustard).
8. Serve with fresh fingers of white bread and butter. A delicious, dry Australian white wine would be most appropriate. And for a special treat, try the oysters with a small glass of very dry sherry.

About Crayfish. Crayfish are the Australian equivalent (almost) to the lobster. In fact their tails are airlifted to some American restaurants and sold as lobster. The crayfish is found in most ocean waters off Australia., Crayfish do not have the huge pincers that Lobsters from North America have, their shells tend to be very rough and jagged, and the pincers are longer and narrower. To make up for this, the rest of the legs of the crayfish probably have a little more meat in them than the lobster. They are equally as expensive as their North American cousins.

Batter-Fried Goodies

Potato Cakes (1)

½ teaspoon salt
1½ cups self-rising flour
½ teaspoon pepper
½ pound boiled potatoes
30 g. (1 oz.) butter
milk to moisten

Sift dry ingredients together and rub in butter. Mash potatoes well. Mix with flour and milk to make a stiff dough. Roll out and cut into rounds about 1 cm thick. Fry in hot pan until brown on both sides.

Potato Cakes (2)

250 g. (½ lb.) potatoes, peeled
1 recipe batter (Fish and Chips)
oil for frying

Parboil potatoes. Remove, drain and allow to cool sufficient to cut into slices about 1 cm thick. Dip each slice in batter, then fry in hot pan until golden brown on each side.

Rice Fritters

2 eggs
1 cup boiled rice
2 teaspoons parsley finely chopped
salt and pepper
batter (Fish and Chips)
oil for frying
spaghetti sauce

Beat eggs well, add rice, parsley, pepper and salt, mix well then shape into patties. Dip in batter and fry in a hot pan until golden brown. Serve with warm spaghetti sauce. **Variation:** Substitute 1-2 tablespoons finely chopped pineapple for parsley.

Prawn (Shrimp) Pie

Crust

1 cup crushed crackers
¼ cup water
100 g. (3 oz.) butter, melted
Combine all ingredients until stiff dough is formed, then press into a greased pie pan. Chill.

Filling

2 tablespoons fresh celery (or, 1 teaspoon celery powder or seeds)
1 onion
1 can cream of oyster soup
1 cup small shrimp
3 eggs
1 cup milk

1. Sauté onion in a little oil, stir in soup.
2. Remove from heat.
3. Beat eggs and milk, add to soup mixture.
4. Stir in shrimp and celery powder, and spoon into pie case.
5. Bake in moderately slow oven (150C, 325F) for 40-50 minutes.

Fish Casserole

500 g. (1 lb.) cooked smoked cod
1 small sliced onion
60 g. (2 oz.) butter
2 hard boiled eggs
1 cup cooked peas
1 small can sweet corn

1. Bone and flake cod and remove skin.
2. Sauté onion in butter and set aside.
3. Make sauce then fold in all other ingredients, cod last so that it does not break up.
4. Spoon into casserole and sprinkle with bread crumbs.
5. Bake in moderate oven (180) until hot and topping is crisp.

Sauce

60 g. (2 oz.) butter
cayenne pepper
4 tablespoons plain flour
1¼ cups milk

1. Melt butter, stir in flour and cayenne pepper, and cook for 1 minute.
2. Gradually add milk, stirring until thick.

Chicken Cairns Supreme

1 Kg (2 lb.) chicken pieces
60 g. (2 oz.) plain flour
60 g. (2 oz.) butter
2 slices bacon
1 large chopped onion
1 cup chopped celery
1 large can cream of chicken soup
4 tablespoons cream
toasted almonds

1. Remove skin from chicken and dust with flour.
2. Fry bacon and onion in butter until cooked but not brown.
3. Arrange chicken pieces in casserole dish.
4. Cover with bacon, onion and can of soup.
5. Cover and bake 35 minutes, 190C.
6. Mix thoroughly celery and cream, top with toasted almonds.
7. Bake a further 10-15 minutes.

Chicken or turkey leftovers may be used in this recipe. In this case, simply arrange leftovers in casserole, cover with soup, bacon and sautéed onion, and heat. Add celery and cream before serving.

About Cairns. Cairns is a large tourist city in the north of Queensland, gateway to the Great Barrier Reef, a coral reef of spectacular beauty, and thousands of miles long. The city was established in 1873 and named after the Governor of Queensland (1875-1877), Sir William Wellington Cairns. It is a city of particular interest to Older Australians and to Americans of similar vintage, for it was here that there was an important air base during World War II.

Chicken Pie

1¼ Kg. (1½ lb.) chicken
2 carrots and 1 onion
1 cup plain flour
1 pound pastry
90 g. (3 oz.) butter
3 slices bacon
2 stems parsley
bay leaves
freshly ground pepper
Pastry from *Maisie's Pasties*.

1. Place chicken in pan with vegetables, bay leaves, parsley, peppercorns and about 10 cm. of water.
2. Bring to boil and simmer for about 1 hour.
3. Strain off liquid and make up to 1¼ cups with water if necessary.
4. Discard vegetables and herbs.
5. Skin chicken and carve flesh into thick slices, removing all meat from bones.
6. Melt butter and fry bacon, set aside.
7. Add flour to butter and cook for 2 minutes.
8. Add liquid, stirring constantly until it comes to boil, then cook for 2 minutes.
9. Season with freshly ground black pepper, and salt to taste.
10. Add carved chicken and bacon, cover and allow to cool.
11. Roll out pastry. Line large pie pan and pour chicken filling in pastry.
12. Cover with pastry, and decorate with strips of pastry trimmed from edge, made into a lattice. Brush with beaten egg and cook in oven 190C (375F) for 1 hour. Eat hot or cold.

About Chicken in Australia. Chicken is not as widely eaten in Australia as in the United States, although it is becoming more and more popular, though it's not as cheap as in America. Chicken pies are not all that common, though they are available in most supermarkets. Certainly, they're no match for Aussie meat pies. **American equivalent:** Chicken pot pies available in supermarkets.

Aussie Chicken Maryland

1 chicken
2 bananas
2 potatoes
½ cup sweet corn
2 eggs
½ cup seasoned flour
2 cups bread crumbs

1. Cut chicken into sections and par-boil.
2. When cold, roll in seasoned flour, egg and bread crumbs.
3. Fry in pan until cooked and outside is crisp and golden.
4. Cook potatoes and mash well.
5. Bind sweet corn with egg and bread crumbs.
6. Cut bananas into four and roll in egg and bread crumbs.
7. Fry bananas and corn until golden brown.

Sauce

4 tomatoes
½ onion
1 piece of bacon or 1 teaspoon cooking oil
ham bone
2½ cups beef bouillon
1½ teaspoons corn flour
salt and pepper

1. Heat oil and sauté onion until transparent, add finely chopped tomatoes and cook 5 minutes.
2. Add stock, bacon bone, salt and pepper, and simmer 1 hour. Remove from heat and puree.
3. Blend corn flour with a little water, then add to mixture. Stir well and cook another 2 minutes.
4. Colour and flavour with soy sauce if desired.
5. Serve chicken pieces on large platter, with banana and corn arranged between pieces. Pipe mashed potato around edge of platter.

Variations: Substitute pineapple pieces or apple slices for the sweet corn. Chicken Maryland is obviously an American dish, given its name. Yet this is one of the oldest chicken recipes one will find in Australia and was once the popular dish for special occasions, featured on the menus of better pub restaurants.

Apricot Chicken

750 g. (1½ lb.) chicken pieces
1 cup apricot nectar (juice)
1 packet French onion soup
10 dried apricots

1. Place chicken into a shallow casserole.
2. Sprinkle soup powder over, then pour on apricot juice.
3. Cook in oven 160C (325F) for 1 hour.
4. 10 minutes before serving, add chopped dried apricots.

About Aussie chicken (chooks). Why chickens are called "chooks" in Australia, I have no idea. Keeping a few chooks in the back yard was once a common practice. They cost little to feed, eating many of the nuisance pests (grubs) in the garden, their dung (in limited quantities) used for fertilizer, and they were a source of a few fresh eggs each day. Chooks used to contribute to the rich sounds of Australian suburbia. Their constant clucking was a comforting sound, heard when one wandered through the fence-lined suburbs of city and small town alike. The day of sound began early with the cries of roosters from the back yards of hundreds of houses. Unfortunately, we no longer hear these sounds because keeping chooks in the back yard is now against the law in Australian cities. Instead, one must be content with the warbling of magpies from the tops of lamp posts, and in smaller towns, the kookaburras cackling in the evening.

Chinese Fowl

1 chicken
6 small mushrooms
2 cups Chinese sausages (chopped)
2 Chinese pickled cucumbers (chopped)
2 tablespoons Chinese gin
2 tablespoons soy sauce
½ teaspoon sugar
¼ teaspoon mixed spices
¼ teaspoon ginger

1. Rub fowl over with soy sauce.
2. Mix all ingredients and stuff chicken.
3. Roast in moderate oven (190C) 1-2 hours, depending on size of chicken.
4. For an added treat, peel and slice potatoes as for French fries. Rub over with soy sauce, fry lightly, add to chicken half hour before serving.

Chinese Australian? You betcha! There is are old and well established Chinese communities in all major Australian cities, most having come to Australia during the gold rush of 1851. Chinese cooks were common on the goldfields:

Celestial is the way he works
The frying-pan and pot.
A splendid feed can be produced
While you'd be counting three,
By the Mandarin from China
That keeps company with me.
—*The Mandarin from China* by Alexander Forbes, 1869

Other Asians were imported for cheap labour in Australia's sugar cane state, Queensland, also in the 19th century.

Rabbit Pie

If you would like to eat rabbit, pretending that it's chicken, then this is the dish for you.

1 boiled rabbit
1½ cups chicken broth
3 tablespoons butter
5 tablespoons plain flour
¾ cup evaporated milk
1 cup diced carrot
1 cup cooked peas (cooked)
6 small white onions
bread crumbs
grated cheese
salt and pepper

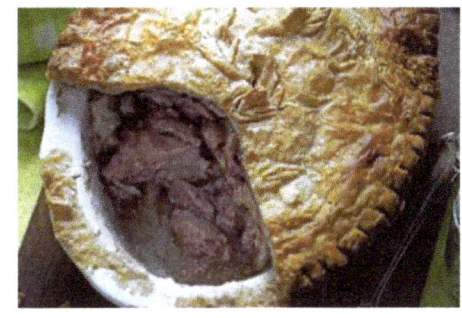

1. To prepare rabbit, see **Jugged Hare.**
2. Cut meat into small pieces.
3. Make a white sauce using butter, flour, evaporated milk and broth.
4. Fold in meat, carrot, peas and onions. Season.
5. Fill oven proof dish.
6. Cover with bread crumbs and cheese.
7. Bake in hot oven (200C, 400F) for 20 minutes. Brown top under broiler as necessary.

About rabbit: Rabbits are yet another gift from the English who settled Australia. In the 20th century, rabbits almost ate Australia, there were so many of them. Many methods were used to reduce their population. One was to conduct a "rabbit drive," often organized by a local church group, in which you begin on a cockey's (farmer's) property, form a long line of people, and make lots of noise. All the rabbits run ahead and are captured in a corner of the paddock fenced off by a rabbit-proof fence.

Ragout of Rabbit

1 rabbit
1 onion
1 slice bacon
2 cups water
2 tablespoons flour
2 tablespoons oil
1 teaspoon salt
pepper
mixed herbs

1. Wash rabbit in warm water and cut into sections.
2. Roll in flour, pepper and salt.
3. Peel and slice onion.
4. Heat oil in pan, then fry rabbit on high heat, both sides. Set rabbit aside.
5. Place onion in pan and fry with flour that remains. When brown, add water, bacon and herbs.
6. Bring to boil, add rabbit then simmer for 1 ½ hours.

To skin a rabbit see **Jugged Hare**. In Australia it is possible to buy rabbits whole, or in pieces, deep frozen. Rabbit should be soaked in salt water for about 11 hours before cooking, to ensure that they are thoroughly clean. After soaking, wash with clean water, and cut off tail and a little of the backbone. Many rabbit dishes use bacon. This is not to mask the flavour (which is succulent, and similar to chicken, if properly cooked), but to make up for the extreme leanness of wild rabbit flesh. Farm raised rabbit (horrors!) will be less lean so may not need the bacon. Wild rabbit is a healthy meat, by all accounts.

Rabbit Mushroom Casserole

1 rabbit
½ cup mushrooms
125 g. (4 oz.) bacon
60 g. (2 oz.) butter
1 tablespoon flour
1 tablespoon parsley (chopped)
salt and pepper
2 tablespoons tomato paste
¼ cup grated cheese
1 cup chicken broth

1. Cut rabbit into serving portions.
2. Melt butter in a pan.
3. Roll rabbit pieces in salt, pepper and flour. Fry in butter until brown, both sides.
4. Allow to cool, then wrap each piece in bacon, securing with a tooth pick.
5. Empty into casserole, add chicken broth, tomato paste and sliced mushrooms.
6. Cook in moderate oven (180C, 350F) for 2 hours. If needed, thicken juice with a little corn flour and arrowroot.
7. Serve topped with grated cheese and parsley.

About rabbits in Australia. As cute as rabbits are, they have been a serious pest just about everywhere in Australia. They have competed for the limited amount of grass with Australia's sheep (who have traditionally had first priority), not to mention Australia's indigenous grass eaters, the kangaroos. There are also hares in Australia, though not so many (see *Jugged hare).* These tend to be much larger than the common grey rabbit, usually more brown in colour.

6

The Aussie Melting Pot

Australia, the Timeless Land is not timeless when it comes to eating. The eating habits of Australians have changed, and are changing rapidly. The Australian continent is about the same size as the continental United States, yet its population is only 23 million. Australia's scarce resource is people, and successive governments have responded to this scarcity by well-orchestrated immigration programs. Today, there is a tremendous variety of peoples living in Australia's cities. In fact, Melbourne (capital of the State of Victoria) is the third largest Greek speaking city in the world. The influence on Australia's restaurants, therefore, by peoples from the Mediterranean, and more recently from parts of the Pacific Islands and South East Asia, is considerable. It is only a matter of time until the cooking traditions of these countries seep into the traditional Australian kitchens, though they are already well established in Aussie pub restaurant menus.

Included in this chapter are recipes in which these cultures' influence is clearly identifiable. Also included in this chapter are vegetarian dishes that would have been very rare in old Australia, a nation of meat eaters. However, influence from the United States and other parts of the world, particularly in regard to health choices and the campaigning of animal rights (led by Australian philosopher-activist Peter Singer) has made vegetarian eating now more or less "OK."

Also included in this chapter are stews, casseroles and curries (both meat and meatless) all of which nestle very well into Australia's traditional way of life because they allow for an informal eating style. They are most often cooked for occasions when there are large family get-togethers, or for social gatherings, where the casserole can be placed at centre table, and dinner served in "smorgasbord" fashion. If presented in this way, they provide no difficulty for the American guest. But should they be served in a formal, sit down dinner style, then the American guest may be in for a bit of a problem.

In fact, any formal dinner makes for a problem for Americans eating in Australia. The reason is that Americans don't hold their knife and fork properly. In an informal smorgasbord style, the American way of eating a casserole type of dish, using the fork in one's dominant hand, collecting the food onto the concave surface of the fork is quite O.K. But in a formal dinner, this is unacceptable because the knife must be held in the right hand (whether dominant or not) and the fork in the left. To make matters even more difficult, the fork must be held with the concave side down which means that there is a definite limit on how much food one can press onto the fork. Managing a plate full of casserole and vegetables requires a lot of practice. However, in some respects, casseroles are a good place to start, because usually there is enough food with some body or absorbent texture (potatoes are very useful). One can push food that might normally fall off the fork (peas, for example) first into the potato, then on to the fork. Learning to use a knife and fork is also easier with a casserole type food because no cutting is required. The drawbacks to eating a casserole with a knife and fork are the juice and gravy. Fortunately, Australians don't mind if you use bread (spread with butter of course) to soak up the remaining gravy. You might even get away with mopping up the gravy with bread held in hand. The more acceptable way would be to place the entire slice of bread and butter on your dinner plate, then cut it up into small pieces with your knife and fork.

Americans have been observed holding the fork gripped in the palm of their hand, as though they were about to use it in an Agatha Christie murder scene! The fork must be held in the left hand, pointer finger running down on top of the fork handle, thumb to the side, other fingers curled around and under. The end of the fork pushes up against the palm of the hand. The concave side of the fork is always facing down. It takes a lot of practice to cut steak like this.

One might add that a sign of decadence in Australian society, is a definite tendency on the part of young Aussies (and even older ones) to use the fork in the right hand, very much in American style, especially when eating rice and other Asian style stir fries, or when eating spaghetti. Presumably this is a result of the slow but sure influx of Italian pastas and Asian stir fries into the Aussie menu. Of course these are necessary changes. If you have tried to eat spaghetti with a knife and fork, held in the "correct" manner, you will understand how difficult it is!

The old ways and traditions are quickly disappearing. It is claimed that three quarters of the children of immigrants in Australia marry outside their own culture. In the 1950s, 80 percent of the population was white European, largely of English stock and this proportion continues to steadily decline. With his constant change, new cooking traditions arise, and many old traditions are adapted to new tastes. So this chapter has a blend of old and new, but even with old recipes, we see the influence of other cultures. Strictly speaking, Australia is a land made up almost entirely of immigrants, if we include in these our forefathers who came from England over the last two centuries. Finally Australia's indigenous peoples remain a minority, but in recent years some of their "bush tucker" has been incorporated into trendy or off beat restaurants. Those dishes have been saved for the final chapter on outback cooking.

Jackaroo Chops

1 kg. (2 lb.) lamb chops
2 tablespoons plain flour
1 teaspoon sugar
6 tablespoons ketchup
4 tablespoons Worcestershire sauce
2 tablespoons vinegar
1 cup water
salt and pepper

1. Remove fat from chops, roll in flour with sugar, salt and pepper.
2. Mix all liquid ingredients together and pour over meat.
3. Bake in a moderate oven (190C, 375F) about 1 hour.

Jackaroo (Jillaroo). A Jackaroo is a station hand, usually on a large station in the Outback. In folk poetry, he is often of "good breeding" and lives with the station hands in order to gain experience:

When you get on to the station, of small things you'll make a fuss,
And in speaking of the station, mind, it's we, and ours, and us.
Boast of your grand connections and your rich relations, too,
And your own great expectations, Jimmy Sago, Jackeroo.
When the boss wants information, on the men I'll do a sneak,
And don a paper collar on your fifteen bob a week*.
Then at the lamb-marking a boss they'll make of you
Oh that's the way to get on, Jimmy Sago, Jackaroo!
  --Jimmy Sago, Jackaroo, Anonymous.

*"bob" is slang for "shillings" used long before Australia changed to decimal currency. The amount here is worth about $1.50

Glazed Pork Fillets

4 pork fillets
¼ cup tomato sauce
¼ cup honey
2 teaspoons soy sauce
¼ teaspoon five spice powder
¼ teaspoon crushed garlic

1. Combine the glaze ingredients and warm in a microwave for 30 seconds.
2. Mix well then pour over the pork fillets in a glass dish.
3. Leave stand for 1 hour.
4. Barbecue or oven bake until the desired level of doneness.

Glaze may be brushed on meat during cooking. This glaze can be kept in the refrigerator in a sealed container for a period of time and used on other pork cuts, such as chops, ham steaks or ribs.

Variation: Sweet and Sour Apricot Sauce
½ cup dried apricots
1 shallot chopped
½ cup white vinegar
⅓ cup honey
¼ cup ketchup
½ teaspoon soy sauce
2 tablespoons oil
1 cup water

1. Combine apricots and water in a pan and bring to boil, reduce heat. Simmer until tender, 15 minutes.
2. Put apricots into the blender, blend until smooth.
3. Return apricots to pan with other ingredients.
4. Bring to the boil, reduce heat and simmer for 5 minutes.
5. Serve with pork or chicken portions from the barbecue.

This sauce keeps very well in the refrigerator in a screw topped jar. Delicious hot or cold. Makes 2 cups
About five spice powder. Used in much oriental cooking, this powder is made up of Star Anise, Cinnamon, Cloves, Fennel and Pepper. It has a distinctive, but mild aniseed flavour.

Fruit Chops Mildura

6 pork loin chops
½ cup pineapple juice
½ cup honey
¼ cup brown sugar
6 maraschino cherries
4-6 whole cloves
6 slices of orange
6 slices of lemon
salt and pepper
1 teaspoon mustard (optional)

1. Brown chops on both sides in buttered pan until almost cooked, add salt and pepper.
2. Combine pineapple juice, honey, brown sugar, mustard and cloves.
3. Place chops in large flat casserole, pour liquid over chops.
4. Gently cook in oven preheated to 190C (375F), for a further 10 minutes. Be careful not to overcook, or chops may become tough.
5. Before serving, attach to each chop a slice of orange, lemon and top with cherry (use a toothpick). Best served with boiled fluffy rice, and a dry white wine.

"Mildura," an Aboriginal word, means "red earth," which is certainly the colour of the land surrounding this large town in the North West of the state of Victoria (the Southern tip of Australia). The area is renowned for its citrus orchards and vineyards. The use of fresh fruits, especially citrus and tropical fruits has become a distinctive part of Australia's cuisine. To old Australians, however, Mildura's main claim to fame is its Working.an's Club (built in 1938) which at the time boasted the longest bar in the world. Pubs (hotels and bars) were prohibited in Mildura early in the 20th century, so private clubs were formed.

Prune Steak

1 kg)2 lb.) choice steak
1-2 tablespoons butter
1 cup flour
1 cup prunes
3-4 peeled tomatoes
1 large onion, sliced
2 tablespoons lemon rind
¼ cup plum jam
1 teaspoon soy sauce
2 tablespoons vinegar
1¼ cups water
chives and parsley
salt and pepper

1. Slice steak into large squares, season with salt and pepper, pound with meat mallet.
2. Sauté onion in large pan until soft; remove and keep warm. In same pan.
3. Brown meat quickly on both sides; remove and keep warm.
4. Sprinkle flour into pan, brown, blend in water. Stir in soy sauce, vinegar and jam.
5. Boil, stirring constantly, until mixture thickens. Return onions and meat to pan, add prunes and lemon rind.
6. Cover and simmer gently for 30-40 minutes until steak is tender. Arrange tomato around in wedges and heat through. Sprinkle with parsley and chives when serving.

If you are not convinced that steak has a very definite place in the Australian menu, an observation made by the children's story writer, Beatrix Potter will dispel any doubts:

> The shearers evidently work very hard... and they live very well -- five meals a day, at three of which they have hot meat.... they get... 20 [shillings] a week, and rations -- 10 [pound] of meat, 10 [pound] of flour, 2 [pound] sugar and 1 [pound] tea per man per week.

--Beatrix Potter in *The Webbs' Australian Diary*, October 9, 1898.

Aussie Beef Ragout

750 g. (1½ lb.) cubed steak
½ cup beef bouillon
3-4 slices lean bacon
2 potatoes peeled and sliced
2 onions peeled and sliced
2 carrots peeled and sliced
1 cup peeled tomatoes
½ cup red wine*
60 g. (2 oz.) butter
¼ cup flour
salt and pepper

1. Roll steak cubes in flour.
2. Cut bacon into large pieces and lightly fry in butter.
3. Remove the bacon then add meat and sauté until browned.
4. Chop tomatoes into large pieces.
5. Butter a casserole dish and place alternate layers of vegetables and meat.
6. Combine claret and stock and pour over casserole.
7. Bake covered for 2½ hours in a moderate oven (180C).
8. Boiled rice or lightly mashed potatoes are excellent companion dishes for this classic meal.

About red wine in Australia. In the 1960s "claret" was probably the first of Australia's wines to receive popular Australian recognition (in contrast to international recognition, where Australia's wines of many types have done well in recent years.) However, the name was a British term used to describe Australia's dry red wines that were something like the French Bordeaux. In fact most of them were probably cabernet sauvignon. It took quite a while for wine to become an acceptable drink in Australia. For many years, the Australian beer drinking tradition frowned upon the drinking of wine, a drink only imbibed by women, or, if by men, they were considered "wino's" or alcoholics. Today, Australia's wine making has come into its own, with corresponding enthusiastic consumption by Australians. The wines are of all varieties, excellent quality, and reasonably priced, and the wineries are everywhere throughout Australia's countryside.

Hamburger Hot Pot

There are many Australian recipes that derive from the English "hot pot" recipes. .

4 potatoes, peeled
¼ pound mozzarella cheese, sliced
500 g. ground beef (minced meat)
1 chopped onion
2 cups canned tomatoes
60 g. (2 oz.) butter

1. Melt butter and cook ground beef quickly over a hot burner.
2. Add tomatoes, onion, salt and pepper to taste.
3. Grease a casserole with margarine and empty ⅓ of the hamburger mixture into casserole, then cover with half the sliced potato.
4. Add another layer of meat mixture and potato then cover with mozzarella cheese slices.
5. Bake in pre-heated oven (170C, 360F) for 1 hour.

Betsy's Porcupines

750 g. (1½ lb.) ground beef (mine meat)
1 egg
1 small chopped onion
½ cup uncooked rice

1. Mix meat, onion and egg well.
2. Make into small balls and roll in rice.
3. Place in casserole and cook 1 hour in a sauce of ½ cup water and 1 can tomato soup.
4. Make sure sauce covers balls while cooking.

About porcupines in Australia. Put simply, there are none. But what Australia does have is the Echidna, a mammal or monotreme, which has stiff spikes or quills just like a porcupine. It is apparently unrelated to the rodent family which is the group ancestor of the North American porcupine. The diet for the Echidna table is termites and other insects it can catch with its long sticky tongue.

Veal and Pineapple Casserole

750 g. (1½ lb.) lean veal
1 can pineapple pieces
   (reserve liquid)
2 onions, sliced
125 g. (4 ounces) lean bacon
¼ teaspoon dried basil

½ cup tomato* juice
½ cup beef bouillon
¼ cup flour
1 tablespoon parsley
   (chopped)
salt and pepper

1. Mix basil with flour.
2. Cut veal into 1 inch pieces and roll in flour and basil.
3. Place half in bottom of well-greased casserole and cover with half the bacon, parsley, onion and pineapple pieces.
4. Add salt and pepper to taste.
5. Repeat layers until no more ingredients are left.
6. Combine ¼ cup pineapple juice, bouillon and tomato juice and pour over casserole.
7. Bake covered for about 2 hours at 175C.

Sweet and Sour Lamb

750 g. (1½ lb.) cubed lamb
1 can pineapple pieces
1 large onion
1 cup diced celery
1 medium pepper (capsicum)
   seeded and sliced

60 g. (2 oz.) butter
2 tablespoons corn flour
2 tablespoons soy sauce
2 tablespoons vinegar
¼ teaspoon pepper
1 teaspoon salt

1. Drain pineapple pieces, make the syrup up to 1 cup of liquid with water and set aside.
2. Sauté pineapple, onion, celery, pepper in half the butter until browned. Remove,, set aside.
3. Add remaining butter and cubed lamb to pan and cook until meat is brown on all sides.
4. Blend corn flour, soy sauce, vinegar, salt and pepper and stir in reserved liquid.
5. Add to meat and cook, stirring until mixture boils and thickens.
6. Cover and simmer for about 50 minutes,
7. Add pineapple and remaining ingredients and cook another 15 minutes. Serve over freshly boiled rice.

Sydney Beef Slice

4 tablespoons tomato puree
¼ cup evaporated milk
¾ cup rolled oats
1 egg
½-1 cup grated cheese
1 teaspoon dry mustard
1 onion finely chopped
500 g. (1 lb.) ground beef (mince meat)
1 4-serve packet instant potatoes

1. Mix in bowl puree, evaporated milk, oats, salt, pepper, egg, mustard and onion.
2. Using large fork or wooden spoon, blend in the ground beef.
3. Grease an 11 by 7 inch pan and spread mixture in base.
4. Bake in pre-heated oven at 190 for 30 minutes.
5. Make up mashed potatoes according to packet directions and add half the grated cheese.
6. Spoon over meat, then sprinkle rest of cheese on top.
7. Bake another 20 minutes.
8. Serve with a brown gravy.

Beef Stew Ballarat*

1 kg (2 lb.) beef cubes
1 large carrot, sliced
1 medium onion, sliced
½ cup mushrooms
¼ cup flour
½ cup stock
½ teaspoon salt
¼ teaspoon pepper
3 slices bacon
1 cup red wine
2 tablespoons tomato paste
1 clove garlic, crushed
½ teaspoon thyme
1 bay leaf

1. Cut bacon into small squares and cook until crisp.
2. Remove from pan and brown beef in bacon fat.
3. Add sliced carrot, onion, salt and pepper, then flour, stirring to coat meat.
4. Add bouillon, wine, tomato paste and herbs. Cover and simmer 2 hours.
5. Cut mushrooms in quarters and sauté in butter. Add to stew.

Ballarat is one of Australia's larger inland cities. It is chiefly known for its historical role in the gold rush years in the 1850s. The world's largest natural gold nugget was found there—the Welcome Nugget.

Irish Stew

500 g. (1 lb.) stewing or braising steak
250 g. (1/2 lb.) onions
1 carrot
1 parsnip

1 kg (2 lb.) potatoes
1 cup water
salt and pepper
chopped parsley

1. Trim fat from meat, cut into 1 inch squares.
2. Place in pan with salt and pepper and cover with water.
3. Peel carrots and onions and cut into slices, add to pan.
4. Bring to boil and simmer for half an hour.
5. Wash and peel potatoes, cut into large pieces and place on top of stew.
6. Sprinkle with salt, place lid on and simmer for 1 hour.
7. Remove any excess fat and serve on plate with meat in centre and potatoes all around. Sprinkle with chopped parsley when serving.

This dish is excellent for cheap cuts of meat.

About the Irish in Australia. Our parents may not have cooked with wine, but they did cook Irish Stew. It is well known that Australia was first settled by convicts. Many of these convicts were Irish.

Lamb Leftovers

500 g. (1 lb.) minced cooked lamb
1 green pepper (capsicum), 1 onion
6 slices lean bacon
1-2 cups prepared stuffing mix
1 egg
1 teaspoon Worcestershire sauce

1. Place green pepper in cold water and bring to boil.
2. Let stand for 3 minutes, then core and chop finely.
3. Combine minced lamb, chopped pepper, chopped onion and stuffing mix, then bind with egg and sauce.
4. Form into round patty shapes about 1 inch thick.
5. Wrap bacon around edges of patties, secure with tooth pick. Place on cookie tray. Heat in moderate oven 180C until bacon is crisp and onion browned.

Sea Pie

This special brown stew has a delicious upper crust topping with a scone-like consistency.

Upper Crust

1 cup plain flour
½ teaspoon baking powder
½ cup shortening
1 pinch salt
water

Sift flour, salt and baking powder, rub shortening into flour until mixture looks like bread crumbs. Mix slowly with water to make a very stiff paste, then knead lightly.

Stew

500 g. (1 lb.) stewing or braising steak, cut in cubes
3 onions
6 potatoes
pepper, salt

1. Sprinkle beef cubes with salt and pepper, place in pan with just enough boiling water to cover. Simmer for 30 minutes.
2. Peel onions and potatoes and cut into small pieces. Add to meat.
3. Roll upper crust dough (above) into a round a little less than the top of the pan.
4. Lay it on the meat, replace pan lid, and cook for a further 1½ hours.
5. When cooked, cut the upper crust in four pieces and place on a warm plate.
6. Arrange the stew on a hot platter and place the crust on top.

Why is it called Sea Pie? This tasty stew is called Sea Pie because it was designed to be cooked at sea, most likely in the sea-faring times when many convicts were transported on many ships from England to Australia. Sailing ships of those times did not have ovens, which means that one could not cook a real pie because a real pie requires pastry to be cooked in an oven. Sea Pie gets around this problem by producing a "crust" that is cooked in the pan.

Greek Pastitsio

1 kg finely minced topside steak, or lean ground beef.
1 chopped onion
2 cloves squashed garlic
2 tablespoons butter
spaghetti

White Sauce
6 tablespoons plain flour
4 tablespoons butter
½ pint milk
4 beaten eggs
120 g.. (4 oz.) grated tasty cheese

1. Simmer onion, garlic, steak in melted butter for 20 min.
2. Cook spaghetti in salted water until al dente, then drain.
3. Grease a large casserole. Put in a layer of spaghetti.
4. Cover with a layer of meat and sprinkle with grated cheese.
5. Continue until all spaghetti and meat is used.
6. Cover with the white sauce and sprinkle with grated cheese.
7. Bake in a moderate to slow oven 160C for 30 minutes. Serves 8-10.

Spaghetti Casserole

500 g. (1 lb.) spaghetti
750 g. (1½ lb.) ground (minced) beef
500 g. (1 lb.) ripe tomatoes
60 g. (2 oz.) butter
1 clove garlic
1 tsp. Worcestershire sauce
1 cup chopped onion
1 cup water
1 cup grated sharp cheese
salt and pepper
1 pinch oregano

1. Sauté crushed garlic and onion in butter until transparent.
2. Add ground beef and brown well. Skin tomatoes.
3. Mix meat with bouillon, sauce, salt, pepper and oregano.
4. Cover and simmer about 15 minutes.
5. Cook spaghetti i until tender but firm. Drain and turn into greased casserole dish.
6. Top with meat mixture, dot with butter and sprinkle with grated cheese.
7. Bake at 170C (350F) until cheese is melted and brown. Garnish with parsley when serving.

Walnut Curry

2 teaspoons of curry powder
750 g. (1½ lb.) stewing or braising steak, cut in cubes
½ cup chopped onion
60 g. (2 oz.) butter
1 banana, sliced
60 g. (2 oz.) chopped walnuts
1 teaspoon salt
2 teaspoons curry powder
1 medium tomato (peeled and diced)
2 cups bouillon

1. Brown meat in butter and remove from pan.
2. Sauté onion and curry powder for 3 minutes.
3. Add banana, tomato, walnuts and beef.
4. Cover with bouillon, add salt and simmer for 1 to 1 ½ hours.
5. When cooked, pour into large warmed tureen, decorate with walnut halves. Serve with fluffy boiled rice.

Curried Spaghetti

125 g. (4 oz.) thin spaghetti
500 g. (1 lb.) ground beef
1 cup chopped onion
1 cup tomato puree
1 cup beef bouillon
2 medium tomatoes, peeled and diced
2 tablespoons dried mushrooms
60 g. (2 oz.) butter
1½ teaspoons curry powder

1. Cook spaghetti in plenty of water for 8 minutes. Drain.
2. Sauté onion and curry powder in butter until onion is transparent.
3. Add meat and cook 5 minutes.
4. Add tomatoes, dried mushrooms, tomato puree and bouillon.
5. Grease casserole and preheat oven to 190C (375F).
6. Place small amount of mixture in base of casserole, empty spaghetti on top, then cover with rest of mixture.
7. Cover and bake 20 minutes.

Queensland Curry

750 g. (1½ lb.) beef cubes
2 onions, chopped
1 green apple, chopped
1 banana, sliced
2 tomatoes, skinned chopped
1 tablespoon curry powder
¼ cup flour

60 g. butter
1 cup pineapple pieces
½ cup coconut
4 tablespoons sultanas
2 tablespoons lemon juice
1¼ cups liquid from pineapple juice and water
salt and pepper

1. Sauté in butter onions, banana, apple, tomatoes and curry powder.
2. Add meat and brown.
3. Add flour and cook 2 minutes, then add liquid, salt and pepper. Bring to boil and simmer 1 ½ hours.
4. Add pineapple pieces, coconut, sultanas and lemon juice.
5. Simmer further 20-30 minutes.
6. Check often for consistency, add liquid if necessary.
7. Serve on bed of boiled rice. Make available an array of nuts (almonds and cashews), carrot sticks, coconut and celery sticks and apple slices to be eaten on the side.

Yogurt Beef Curry

30 g. (1 oz.) butter
2 onions, sliced
1 small clove garlic
750 g. (1½ lb.) beef cubes
½ teaspoon marsala
1 tablespoon curry powder
1 teaspoon turmeric
1 ¼ cups beef bouillon
1 ¼ cups plain yogurt

1. Sauté garlic and onions in butter until transparent.
2. Add steak and continue to cook until meat changes colour.
3. Now add curry powder, marsala and turmeric
4. Sauté 5 minutes. Add salt and bouillon, cover, and simmer about 2 hours or until meat is tender.
5. Add yogurt, stir well and simmer with lid off until most liquid has evaporated.
6. Serve on bed of boiled long grain rice. Provide small dishes of chopped tomato, chopped onions, banana slices, coconut and pineapple pieces.

Potato Curry

4 tablespoons oil
2 onions sliced
4 large potatoes peeled and diced (not too small)
1 cup water
1 can tomatoes, drained
1½ tablespoons coconut milk
½ teaspoon each, ground turmeric, cinnamon, cardamom, black pepper, cumin, ginger, sugar, chili powder and salt.

1. Heat oil, add onion and fry until transparent.
2. Add garlic and potatoes and fry 2 minutes more.
3. Add remaining ingredients, bring to boil and simmer until potatoes are cooked.
4. Add reserved tomato liquid if needed.
5. Serve with boiled rice and a selection of:
   Natural yogurt with diced cucumber and mint
   Bananas sliced in lemon juice
   Pappadums
   Mango chutney
   Pineapple pieces.

Mango and Port Chutney

4 medium mangoes, chopped
¾ cup of port
1 cup chopped raisins
2 teaspoons grated fresh ginger
2 small fresh red chilies, finely chopped
3 cups brown sugar
2 teaspoons yellow mustard seeds

1. Combine mangoes in large pan with all ingredients.
2. Stir constantly over heat without boiling and until sugar is dissolved. Bring to boil, reduce heat.
3. Simmer uncovered for 1 ½ hours or until chutney is thick.
4. Towards end of cooking time, stir occasionally.
5. Pour into hot, sterilized jars. Seal when cold.

Honey Sweet Potatoes

1 kg (2 lb.) sweet potato
100 g. (3 oz.) pecans
60 g. (2 oz.) butter
1 teaspoon grated orange rind
1 cup orange juice
¼ cup honey
cinnamon
chopped chives

1. Peel potato and chop into large cubes.
2. Bring water to boil, add potatoes and cook uncovered until just tender.
3. Drain into a colander and leave stand.
4. Melt butter in the pan, add pecans and cook until lightly browned.
5. Remove pecans and drain on kitchen paper.
6. Add orange rind, orange juice, honey and cinnamon to taste, to butter in pan.
7. Bring to the boil and reduce liquid to half.
8. Add potatoes to liquid and heat through, stirring gently.
9. Sprinkle nuts and chives over the potatoes just before serving.

8

Salads

It is not so much the conglomeration of different vegetables that makes the Australian salad so "typical" but rather the way the salad is served. This reflects a general difference in table manners between Australians and Americans. The American practice of beginning meals with a salad is virtually unknown in Australia. In America, the salad is usually eaten as a meal in itself or kept to the side and eaten along with the main meal. Older Australians when they visit America, are annoyed by this practice. They keep their small dish of salad, then empty it on to the main dish when it's served!

If you would prefer less formality (which is more Australian, actually) you might like to pack up your salad plates and head for the beach. In this case, choose your largest icebox (called a car fridge or "Esky" in Australia), carefully lay out the salad on separate disposable plates (strong ones so they won't absorb too much moisture and bend in two when you lift them out), cover with plastic wrap, and place in your icebox along with a plentiful supply of cold beer for the men (!) and soft drinks (soda) for the kids, and separately, a couple of thermos flasks of tea (for everyone). Tea kept this way doesn't taste right unless prepared properly: see **cuppa tea.** A few sandwiches and slices of plain bread and butter will also go down well. Then fill a container with a selection of cookies.

Now you're ready for a day on the beach. Load the boot of your car (trunk to Americans) with a cricket bat and ball, a large sun hat and sun screen, and you're in for a relaxing sun-drenched day in the healthy salt air. Ah! the fine white and beige sand sifting through the toes... the gently swaying grass on the dunes... the sheer red cliffs facing the sea... A day can pass very easily swimming in the crystal water of Australia's surf beaches, playing cricket on the sand. These activities do wonders for the appetite—you need to have a big icebox. Australia is blessed with thousands of miles of sandy beaches, only a tiny portion of them "developed" in the sense that they are patrolled, have car parks and so on. Laws will not allow individuals to own or build up to the ocean shore line. Australians who travel abroad—whether to Europe or the United States—are aghast that one would either have to pay to get on to a beach, or that individuals could actually own land and houses right down to the water. The drive down Big Sur in California, while stunning in its own right, to an Australian seems defaced because of the houses (no matter how beautiful) built right down to the shore line.

If you would like to serve your Australian salad in surroundings without sand but retaining the Aussie style, be sure to set your table with a "bread and butter plate" for each guest. Just about every Australian meal is served with bread and butter, Australian salads especially. The Australian bread and butter plate is about the size of a small plate that Americans would use for salad.

Ingredients of an Australian Salad
- firm tomatoes thinly sliced
- short celery sticks
- grated carrot
- thinly sliced cucumber
- beet root
- thinly sliced orange
- thin slices of banana
- one or two pieces of apple
- fresh pineapple squares
- fresh whole lettuce leaves
- parsley
- grated cheese
- cold cooked peas
- cold cooked string beans
- small boiled baby potatoes (cold with butter)
- sliced boiled egg
- gherkins
- pickled onions
- canned salmon
- raisins
- avocado
- potted meat

Use as wide a variety of fresh garden vegetables as you can find. The Australian salad is most often served with a few thin slices of cold cuts, such as roast beef, ham, German sausage or chicken, and a little potted meat (see **potted steak**). Naturally, these cold dishes are most popular in summer time in Australia, when it's not unusual to have Christmas dinner on the beach. The cold cuts are usually arranged flat on one side of the plate, nestling against various ingredients, with crisp lettuce on the outside of the plate. Thin slices of orange, split and twisted are common—intended to be eaten as well as for decoration.

Victoria Salad

6 medium tomatoes
salt, pepper and sugar
cup grated cheese
1 tablespoon finely chopped pineapple and nuts
cup lettuce, finely chopped
1 teaspoon parsley, finely chopped
1 teaspoon chopped scallions (spring onions)

1. Cut off tops of tomatoes and scoop out centres, sprinkle with salt, pepper and sugar.
2. Mash the tomato pulp well and mix in cheese, pineapple and nuts, parsley, scallions and lettuce.
3. Fill cases with mixture, sprinkle top with cayenne pepper. Top with a small daub of thick mayonnaise.
4. Set each tomato on a crisp lettuce leaf. Serve chilled.

Don't forget the bread and butter.

Golden Salad

1 can pineapple rings
250 g. (½ lb.) cheddar cheese
4 medium tomatoes, firm
6 radishes
1 lettuce
French or Italian dressing

1. Cut the cheese into small cubes, the tomatoes into wedges, and radishes into roses.
2. Tear lettuce into pieces and place in salad bowl.
3. Arrange pineapple rings in circle, tomato wedges around edge.
4. Place cheese cubes in centre, radish rose in each pineapple ring.
5. Garnish with a few mint leaves. Add dressing to taste.

Joan's Pacific Salad

fluffy boiled rice
grated carrot
pineapple bits and some juice
currants
sultanas
chopped tops of scallions (spring onions)
cooked peas
chopped nuts (optional)
coconut (optional)

1. Mix all ingredients, varying amounts according to taste.
2. Serve on large shallow dish, surrounded by orange and lemon slices.

Coconut Salad

2 peeled and chopped oranges
250 ml can (8 oz.) crushed pineapple
100 g. (3 oz.) shredded coconut
⅓ cup cultured sour cream

1. Combine oranges and drained pineapple in a clear salad bowl. Add shredded coconut and sour cream.
2. Mix all ingredients , decorate with a curled slice of orange or finely shredded orange peel. Serve immediately.

Green and Gold Salad

1 cucumber thinly sliced
1 can mandarin seg.ents well drained, peeled and sliced
3 bananas, 2 pears, 2 avocados (sliced)
Lettuce leaves
Chutney Dressing
  ½ cup mayonnaise   dash of Tabasco
  ½ cup sour cream   4 tablespoons oil
  4 tablespoons chutney   2 tablespoons white wine vinegar,
  ¼ teaspoon curry powder   pinch salt

1. Arrange lettuce leaves in large salad bowl, and place fruit and vegetables in a pattern of green and gold.
2. Mix chutney dressing and serve in small dish placed in centre of bowl. Best prepared as close to eating time as possible.

Queensland Salad

2 avocados, peeled & sliced
2 mangoes, peeled & sliced
⅓ cup chopped nuts (pecans or walnuts)
2 bacon rashers, chopped
1 lettuce (mignonette, radichio etc.)

Dressing
¼ cup olive oil
4 tablespoons lemon juice
2 tablespoons thickened cream
1 teaspoon mustard (mild)

1. Combine all dressing ingredients in a jar and shake well.
2. Cook chopped bacon in a pan until crisp.
3. Drain on kitchen paper.
4. Arrange avocado, mango, nuts, and bacon over a bed of lettuce. Top with dressing. Make close to eating time.

Cauliflower and Beetroot Salad

1 small cauliflower
2 small fresh beets
2 eggs
¼ pound goat cheese

1. Boil the cauliflower and beetroot separately. Leave till cold.
2. Divide cauliflower into small sprigs, and cut beets into thin strips.
3. Cut cheese into small cubes. Boil eggs hard. Chop the white and rub yolk through a sieve.
4. Make a border of cauliflower on a dish.
5. Fill centre with beetroot strips mixed with cheese and chopped egg white.

Pour the dressing over and sprinkle with egg yolk.

Dressing

6. Stir yolk of an egg vigorously while adding 2 tablespoons of oil, drop by drop. S
7. Stir in 2 tablespoons of thick cream, and add by degrees a teaspoon of vinegar and pinch of salt and pepper.

Sunshine Salad

1 250 ml (89 oz.) can of crushed pineapple
1 cup grated carrot
½ cup of chopped celery
1 lemon Jell-O (jelly), water
½ teaspoon mustard,
4 tablespoons vinegar

1. Drain pineapple, reserve syrup and add vinegar and mustard.
2. Make up to ½ litre with water.
3. Dissolve Jell-O in the liquid allow to cool then add pineapple, carrot and celery.
4. Pour into a flat glass dish and set in the fridge.
5. Cut into squares for ease of serving.

9

Cookies and Slices

Cookies and tasty slices are made for all occasions in Australia, for entertaining, and to have around for the kids to stave off their constant hunger.

Australians have a casual lifestyle, and an enviable openness in their social life. A typical way to spend the weekend is to "drop in" on friends and rellies (relatives). This means what it says. One may be visited by people without warning. Many Australian households keep a constant supply of cookies and slices that can be produced, along with a cup of tea, for unexpected guests. An easy solution to this pleasant, but demanding custom, would be to serve bought cookies. However, as the English say, this simply would not do. The cookies and slices are often the focus of conversation, and it may be at this time that new recipes are exchanged and discussed.

Cookies are most often served in the morning at "morning tea" (around 10.30 a.m.) at which time everything stops. Most places of work sound a whistle or bell (in factories, schools, universities and government departments) when it is time to break for tea.

Anzac Biscuits (Cookies)

Mothers used to make these chewy mouth-watering cookies every few weeks, not especially on ANZAC day. One dreams of their treacle flavour.

¾ cup fine sugar
¾ cup coconut
½ cup treacle
1 cup flaked oatmeal
¼ pound butter
¾ cup plain flour
1 teaspoon baking soda
2 tablespoons boiling water

1. In saucepan place butter, treacle, soda, sugar and mix with boiling water.
2. Bring slowly to boil, remove and add dry ingredients, mixing well.
3. Place large spoonfuls of mixture about 3 inches apart on a well-greased cookie tray.
4. Bake in slow oven (150C, 300F) for 25 minutes.

About Aussie Cookies. Not many Australians use the word "cookie." All cookies are "biscuits" to Australians. And what Americans call "biscuits" Australians call "scones" (see **scones**). Generally speaking, Australian cookies are drier and less chewy than American cookies. ANZAC biscuits are an exception.

About ANZAC Day. ANZAC day is celebrated in Australia on April 25. On this day in 1915, the ANZACs (Australian and New Zealand Army Corps) landed at Gallipoli, and suffered the worst defeat in Australian military history. The fallen soldiers of all wars are now commemorated on ANZAC Day. ANZAC biscuits, because they were soft, were thought to keep better when shipped across to Australia's troops during World War I. Thus, they came to be called ANZACs.

Afghans

In the Australian holiday season, (Christmas through New Year) Mums everywhere make these chocolate cookies. In a time when the abundance of chocolate can cause chocolate cookie blues, Afghan biscuits (cookies) provide a distinctive chocolate taste that simply does not exist anywhere else.

190 g. (6 oz.) butter
⅓ cup fine sugar
2 tablespoons cocoa
60 g. (2 oz.) cornflakes
¾ cup self-rising flour
⅓ cup plain flour
3-6 drops vanilla
1 pinch salt

1. Cream butter and sugar, add salt and vanilla to taste.
2. Sift dry ingredients then add to mixture, mixing well.
3. Add cornflakes and mix thoroughly.
4. Place on cold greased cookie tray, and bake 15 minutes at 190.
5. These cookies are great plain, but even better topped with just a dollop of chocolate frosting (see *icing*).

Why are they called Afghans? This is a very old recipe. We have no idea how these cookies got their name. They are a dark brown, however, and it's possible that someone in the outback who came across an Afghan and his camel, thought the cookies were the colour of the Afghan (or maybe his camel). Yes, there are camels in the Australian outback. They were introduced in 1840.

Christmas Cookies

At Christmas time, Aussies always do their "Christmas baking" and prepare a variety of tasty morsels that are even more succulent than the usual fare provided at afternoon teas.

Rum Fudge Balls
1 can condensed milk (375 ml)
½ cup coconut
2 tablespoons cocoa
1 cup plain cookies (crushed)
1 teaspoon vanilla
2 tablespoons rum

Mix all ingredients thoroughly together, roll into balls. Cover with coconut, chill in refrigerator. **Variation**: Take slivers of dates and encase them in the above mixture. Roll in chocolate sprinkles, chill.

Choc Balls
1 large packet marshmallows
60 g. (2 oz.) butter
¾ cup condensed milk
¼ cup coconut
3 tablespoons cocoa
1 packet plain cookies

Melt butter and milk slowly. Add cocoa and coconut. Leave to set 5 minutes while you crush the cookies. Add to mixture, mix thoroughly. Roll into small balls, chill.

Apricot Coconut Balls
2 cups dried apricots
1 can (375 ml, 8 oz.) condensed milk
1 cup cornflakes
1 cup coconut

Finely crush the cornflakes. Mince apricots and mix all ingredients well. Roll into balls, cover with coconut, chill.

Coconut Ruffs
1 can (375 ml, 8 oz.) condensed milk
½ pound coconut
1 teaspoon vanilla
2 tablespoons cocoa

Thoroughly mix all ingredients. Place teaspoonfuls on cold cookie tray and bake in oven 190C (375F) for 10 minutes. Keep refrigerated.

Tutty Fruity
>1 can (375 ml, 8 oz.) evaporated milk
>1 passion fruit
>juice of ½ lemon
>1 banana
>juice of 1 orange
>¾ cup sugar

Combine all ingredients, beat thoroughly and pour into flat pan, chill. Cut into small squares for serving.

Fruit Mince Tarts

These and many other types of cookies and slices are very popular in Australia around Christmas time, and are not often served during the rest of the year.

Fruit Mince
>¾ cup chopped raisins
>90 g. (3 oz.) brown sugar
>¼ cup chopped glacé fruits
>2 tablespoons of brandy
>½ teaspoon mixed spice
>½ lemon
>1 grated apple
>90 g. (3 oz.) currants
>¼ cup of mixed peel
>¼ cup of shortening
>½ orange

Mix all ingredients thoroughly.

Tarts
>375 g. (12 oz.) pastry
>egg yolk for glazing
>fruit mince
>confectioners' sugar

1. Use pastry from **Amy Johnston Cake**. Roll out the pastry to about 2 cm. thick.
2. Cut into rounds so that those for the bottoms are slightly larger than those for the tops.
3. Line muffin tins with pastry, spoon in fruit mince.
4. Wet edges of pastry cases, place on tops, and pinch together with sides.
5. Glaze with egg yolk. Bake in hot oven (200C, 400F) for about 10 minutes. Cool on wire rack and dust with sugar.

Marshmallow Slice

6 cups cornflakes
1 cup coconut
1 cup plain flour

500 g. butter
¾ cup brown sugar
1 pinch salt

1. Mix dry ingredients, add melted butter, mix thoroughly.
2. Press with fingers into flat pan.
3. Bake in moderate oven 175 for 15 minutes. Allow to cool.

Glaze

125 g. marshmallow
1 cup sugar
¾ cup water

1-4 drops vanilla
1 tbsp. gelatine (dissolved in hot water)
1 cup chocolate bits (melted)

1. Boil together sugar, water and vanilla.
2. Add gelatine, mix thoroughly, allow to cool.
3. Whip until mixture becomes fluffy.
4. Spread on cookie mixture and top with melted chocolate.

Vanilla Slice

Vanilla slice is a perennial favourite. The centre is a type of thick vanilla custard. We have found slices something similar in American bakeries, but the custard filling is not the same consistency, and as usual, there's too much of it.

125 g. (4 oz.) flaky pastry
¾ cup milk
1 tablespoon sugar
1 egg
1 tablespoon corn flour
1 teaspoon vanilla

1. Use pastry from **Amy Johnston Cake**. Roll out pastry into 2 thin strips of equal size.
2. Prick all over with fork and bake until crisp and golden in hot oven (about 200C, 400F).
3. Blend corn flour with milk and sugar, stir continuously over low heat until boiled and thick.
4. Remove, stir in vanilla and beaten egg. Spread between the 2 strips of pastry (you should have about 1 cm of cream between the two layers of pastry) and frost top with vanilla icing (see **icing**).
5. Cool in refrigerator, cut into 3 cm squares.

Yo Yo Biscuits (Cookies)

An Aussie expatriate dreams at least once a week of these addictive cookies. Aussies cook them about as much as American Moms cook chocolate chip cookies or brownies. These are the blue chip of cookies. Once you have tasted them, you won't rest until you have devoured them all.

60 g. (2 oz.) custard powder
¾ cup butter
½ cup castor sugar
¾ cup plain flour

1. Cream butter and sugar. Sift flour and custard powder 3 times.
2. Mix into butter and sugar and work until a stiff dough is obtained.
3. Roll into small balls about the size of large marbles, or a little bigger.
4. Place each ball on a greased cookie sheet, pressing down on the top of each with the back of a fork.
5. Bake at 175C (350F) for 15 to 20 minutes.
6. When cool, join together in pairs with vanilla frosting (see **icing**).

They look like yo-yo's! And they taste like nothing you have ever tasted before.

About Custard Powder. Custard powder is a mainstay of every Australian kitchen. Hopefully your gourmet food store in America will stock this very useful product, made in England as well as Australia.

Melting Moments

These tasty morsels are nearly the same as Yo-Yos but contain corn flour instead of custard powder, so they are fine for people with egg allergies.

125 g.. (4 oz.) butter
½ cup. castor sugar
¾ cup plain flour
50 g.. (1½ oz.) corn flour

1. Cream butter and sugar.
2. Fold in sifted flour and cornflour.
3. Place teaspoonful on a baking tray and cook in a moderate to slow oven for 15 minutes.
4. Do not join with icing, as in Yo-Yos because these morsels are already sugary enough!

Walnut Delights

1 cup self-rising flour
150 g. (6 oz.) butter
1 egg yolk
1 pinch salt
1 tablespoon fine sugar
1 tablespoon water

1. Rub butter into flour, add sugar.
2. Mix to a stiff dough with egg yolk beaten with a little water.
3. Roll out thin and line greased muffin pans.

Filling
60 g.(2 oz.) butter
½ cup walnuts
1 egg
⅓ cup fine sugar

4. Cream butter and sugar, then add eggs and walnuts (finely chopped).
5. Bake in moderate oven (180C, 365F) for 15 minutes.

Anne's Cherry Ripe

Cherry Ripes are commercial candy bar unavailable in the United States. Here is a home-made version.

250 g. (½ lb.) plain cookies
6 tablespoons shortening
1 tablespoon fine sugar
¾ cup evaporated milk
½ teaspoon red food colouring
½ teaspoon almond essence
¼ cup glazed cherries
1 cup desiccated coconut

1. Grease a 17 by 27 cm. shallow cooking pan, and arrange a layer of cookies in base.
2. Melt shortening and mix in remaining ingredients, blending thoroughly.
3. Spread over cookies and allow to stand for about 1 hour.
4. Place in freezer, remove when frozen and cover with thick layer of chocolate frosting (see **icing**).
5. When thawed, cut into about 3 cm squares.

Dot Bowmans

This recipe comes from the legendary Dot Bowman of Dandenong (Australia).

125 g. (4 oz.) butter
¼ cup sugar
1 cup chopped dates
3 cups rice crispies (rice bubbles)
½ 1 cup chocolate chips, melted

1. Place butter, sugar and dates in saucepan and stir over low heat until a thick paste.
2. Put rice crispies (rice bubble in Australia) in large basin, add date mixture and stir well.
3. Spread in a shallow pan. Cover with melted chocolate.
4. Cool in refrigerator and cut into about 3 cm squares.

About Dandenong. Dandenong is one of our spouse's home town. It's nothing like the name suggests (a sleepy dusty village in the red of the Australian outback). Not at all. It's a bustling city, part of the suburban sprawl of Melbourne (located on the Southeast tip of Australia). Australia folklore authority, Keith McKenry, reports that "Dandenong" is aboriginal for "no good damper" which must be what aborigines many years ago thought of the cooking in this area! (See **Outback Cooking** to find out how to cook damper):

>"Damper wrong! Damper wrong!"
>The toothless blacks all cried,
>Excepting those who'd swallowed some,
>And they laid down and died.
>For what they'd gone and done, you see,
>Though flour had been meant,
>They'd gone and pinched a hundredweight
>Of best Portland cement
>Now over the years that mournful cry
>Of Damper Wrong has changed,
>And this is how the district
>Of Dandenong got its name.

--*How Dandenong Got Its Name*, Keith McKenry, 1970.

Frosted Cherry Rounds

125 g. (4 oz.) butter
⅓ cup coconut
¾ cup plain flour
125 g. fine sugar
2 tablespoons rice flour
1 egg
2 tablespoons crystallized cherries

1. Separate egg yolk and white, sift flour and rice flour; add half the sugar and rub in butter until mixture forms a stiff dough with egg yolk.
2. Turn on to board and knead lightly. Roll out to 1 inch thickness.
3. Cut into rounds with fluted cutter and place on greased cookie sheet.
4. Whip egg white stiffly and add remaining sugar and the coconut.
5. Pipe this mixture on to cookies and top with cherry.
6. Preheat oven to 175C (350F), place in oven, reset oven to 145C (300F) and bake for 20-25 minutes, or until coconut is brown.

Jean's Ginger Slice

This is another prize recipe from Dandenong (pronounced Dan-dee-nong; see **Dot Bowmans**). These slices will keep well, stored in an airtight container in refrigerator.

1¾ cups plain flour
¾ cup butter
¼ teaspoon salt
1 cup fine sugar
½ cup preserved ginger
1 egg

1. Melt butter in saucepan and allow to cool.
2. Add remaining ingredients, mixing thoroughly.
3. Spread in shallow pan and bake in moderate oven (180) for 25 minutes.
4. Allow to cool in pan, cut into slices.

May's Fudge Shortbread

½ cup butter
½ cup sugar
1½ cups plain flour
Beat together butter and sugar. Add flour until mixture is firm enough to roll and put in shallow pan.

125 g. (4 oz.) butter
½ cup fine sugar
4 tablespoons golden syrup
1 cup condensed milk

1. Place all ingredients in basin and beat until creamy.
2. Cook in small saucepan over medium heat, until mixture bubbles.
3. Let cool, spread over shortbread.
4. Allow to cool, then add topping:

60 g. (2 oz.) dark chocolate
30 g. (1 oz.) butter

5. Melt chocolate, add butter and mix thoroughly.
6. Pour over mixture, allow to cool, then cut into slices for serving.

About Golden Syrup. Golden syrup is a by-product of molasses manufacture and is hard to find in America, though should be available at your gourmet food store. A close substitute is 1 part light and 1 part dark corn syrup with some success, although this mixture tends not to have the strong sugary-sweetness of golden syrup.

Lemon (Orange) Fingers

½ cup butter
6 cups coconut
⅓ cup condensed milk
250 g. (½ lb.) plain cookies
rind of 1 orange
1 recipe **lemon icing** for orange frosting

1. Heat butter and condensed milk over low heat.
2. Add to dry ingredients. Mix well. Press into shallow pan.
3. Top with lemon or orange frosting (icing).

Raspberry Sandwiches

¾ cup sugar
½ cup butter
2 cups plain flour
1 teaspoon cream of tartar
½ teaspoon baking soda
1 egg

1. Cream butter and sugar, add egg and beat well.
2. Sift together flour, cream of tartar and baking soda.
3. Add to mixture and mix well.
4. Roll out thin and bake in hot oven (200C, 400F) for 5 to 10 minutes.
5. While hot, cut in two halves and join together with jam.

Burnt Butter Biscuits (Cookies)

2 eggs
1 teaspoon vanilla
1 cup butter
1 cup sugar
1¼ cups self rising (self raising) flour
1 pinch salt
almonds

1. Brown the butter, being careful not to burn it.
2. Allow it to cool then cream with sugar.
3. Add eggs, then vanilla essence, sifted flour and salt.
4. Place small teaspoonfuls on cookie tray, and place half an almond on top of each. Bake 10 minutes at 190C (375F).

Neenish Tarts

½ cup butter
1 teaspoon baking powder
½ cup sugar
1 pinch salt
1 egg
1 cup plain flour

1. Cream butter and sugar, add egg and beat well.
2. Mix in sifted dry ingredients and knead well.
3. Roll out then line greased muffin pans with mixture.
4. Prick with fork and bake 10-15 minutes at 175C (350F).

Prepare filling:
½ butter
½ cup fine sugar
½ cup condensed milk
2 tablespoons lemon juice

5. Soften butter, add sugar, condensed milk and lemon juice.
6. Spoon into patty shells. When set, ice top half with white icing and half with chocolate icing (see **icing**).

Lemon Snaps

1 cup sugar
1 egg
½ cup butter
2 lemons for juice, rind of one
flour to stiffen

1. Mix all ingredients together thoroughly, adding flour to stiffen to desired consistency.
2. Roll out thinly, place on cookie tray and bake in quick oven (200C, 400F)) about 7 minutes.

Roma's Chocolate Velvet

1½ cups finely crushed chocolate cookies
⅓ cup melted butter

1. Mix together and press into 22 by 32 cm flat pan.
2. Bake at 165C (325F) for 10 minutes. Cool.

1 250 g. (½ lb.) cream cheese
1 teaspoon vanilla (or less)
1 180 g. (6 oz.) melted chocolate chips
½ cup sugar
2 eggs
1 cup whipped cream
¾ cup chopped walnuts

3. Combine softened cream cheese, 1 cup sugar and vanilla, mixing well.
4. Stir in beaten egg yolks and chocolate.
5. Beat egg whites until stiff peaks form.
6. Gradually beat in remaining cup of sugar.
7. Fold in whipped cream and nuts; pour over cookie crumbs.
8. Freeze. After frozen, remove and cut into 2-3 cm squares for serving.

Authentic Australian? There's always a question of whether certain recipes are authentically Australian or not, especially because just about everyone in Australia (except the indigenous peoples, and even they came from Asia some 40,000 years ago) came there from some place else. Frankly, this recipe looks very American— the cream cheese is a bit of a give-away.

10

Cakes

Cakes, as with cookies, are kept in constant supply in the Australian kitchen. The necessity to keep cakes and cookies in supply is what sets the Australian kitchen apart from the American. It is usually cluttered with all kinds of containers for storing cakes and cookies. There are different containers for different cakes. Those with pastry in them should not be in completely airtight containers. Light cakes, however, such as sponges need to be completely airtight or they will dry out.

Cakes are most often served for "afternoon tea" which may be had anywhere from 2.00 p.m. to 4.00 p.m. While some work places stop for afternoon tea, it is not a common practice. Afternoon tea is more likely to be served to guests who arrive in the afternoon during a weekend visit. Usually, these guests are invited or expected guests, and baking is done specially in preparation for them.

Afternoon tea is not to be confused with the Scottish practice of taking "High Tea" on Sundays. This is a combined afternoon tea and evening meal, at which are served savories, eggs, toast, along with a variety of cakes and jellies. High tea is not served in Australia. However, to confuse matters, the word "tea time" is used by many Australians, to refer to the evening meal.

Amy Johnston Cake

Pastry, cakes and jam. Put these simple favourites together, top with lemon or vanilla frosting (icing), and you have a delicious cake that will excite the taste buds of even sworn beer drinkers*.

Pastry
½ cup self-rising (raising) flour
60 g. (2 oz.) butter
¼ cup of milk (approx.)
1 jar (300 g.) raspberry jam

1. Rub butter into flour, adding enough milk to make a fairly stiff paste.
2. Roll pastry, place in flat pan and spread with jam.

Cake
1 cup self-rising (raising) flour
1 cup of sugar
60 g. butter
½ cup milk
2 eggs

3. Blend flour and sugar, rub in butter.
4. Stir eggs lightly, add to mixture, blend while adding enough milk to make a smooth consistency, easy to stir but not too thin.
5. Pour over jam and bake 25 minutes at 175C (350F).
6. Top with vanilla or lemon frosting (see **icing**), when cold.
7. Cut into 1 inch squares and serve with English breakfast tea.

Maisie's Chocolate Peppermint Cake

½ teaspoon vanilla
½ cup sugar
2 eggs
½ cup butter
⅔ cup self-rising (raising) flour
4 tablespoons cocoa
water to mix

1. Cream butter and sugar.
2. Add well beaten eggs and vanilla.
3. Fold in flour and cocoa, mixing to a thick creamy consistency by adding water.
4. Place in 22.5 cm cake pan. Bake in moderate oven (175C, 350F) for 30 minutes.
5. When cool, slice and insert filling. Or, better yet cook another one, and place on top of each other, with filling in centre.

Peppermint Filling
30 g. (1 oz.) butter
¼ cup fine sugar
1 tablespoon hot water
1 tablespoon milk
3-6 drops peppermint essence
green colouring

6. Cream butter and sugar, add hot water, mix again, then add milk and green essence.
7. Mix until creamy and smooth.
8. Cover the entire cake with a thick chocolate frosting (see **chocolate icing**).

Helen's Chocolate Cake

80 g.. (3 oz.) butter
1 cup sugar
2 eggs
60 g.. (2 oz.) cocoa powder
1 cup self-rising (raising) flour
½ cup milk

1. Put all dry ingredients in a bowl. Melt butter, add half the milk.
2. Add eggs and melted butter to dry ingredients and beat well.
3. Add rest of the milk as needed until a firm batter is made.
4. Put into a floured and lined cake pan and bake in a moderate oven (180C 370F) for 20 minutes. Press centre of cake to test if cooked.
5. Cool on a wire rack and ice with good chocolate icing. t.

Apple Shortcake

1 cup self-rising (raising) flour
½ cup fine sugar
½ cup butter
1 egg
1 teaspoon each, cinnamon, ginger, & mixed spice.

1. Cream butter & sugar add egg then dry ingredients.
2. Spread mixture into two greased and floured sandwich tins.
3. Do not spread right to the edge and you will get a nice flat top on the cakes.
4. Bake in a moderate oven (180C, 370F) for approx. 30 minutes. They will be light brown and crisp when cooked.
5. The shortcake can be made many days before you wish to use it and only needs 2 hours to soften after filling.
6. Put unsweetened stewed apples between the cakes about 2 hours before serving.
7. Sprinkle top with icing sugar or spread with cream. Other fillings can be used, such as strawberries or pitted prunes folded through whipped cream

Marshmallow Cake

One can understand how it might be assumed that any cake or cookie with marshmallow in it would be as American as apple pie! The difference with this recipe is that you get to make your own marshmallow.

1 egg
½ cup butter
½ cup sugar
1 cup self-rising flour
rind of one lemon, grated

1. Cream butter and sugar, add eggs and rind of lemon.
2. Fold in flour. When thoroughly mixed, press into flat 20 cm. pan and bake at 175C (350F) for 15 minutes or until golden brown.
3. When cold, top with the following:

Marshmallow
1 tablespoon gelatine
1 cup sugar
¾ cup water
lemon juice
toasted coconut

4. Place all ingredients into saucepan, bring slowly to simmer.
5. Allow to cool, place in refrigerator for half an hour or until quite cold.
6. Beat until thick and white, add lemon juice to taste. Spread over cake, top with coconut.

About Marshmallow in Australia. Marshmallow enjoys a warm spot in every expatriate Australian's heart. Most Aussies have never seen snow, but they do know that light fluffy marshmallow in "snowballs" (a ball of marshmallow dipped in chocolate) is whiter than snow, and is one of the memorable Aussie lollies (candy).

Sponge Cake

Long ago, an accomplished cook was judged by how well she could make a sponge cake. These cakes are possibly the most typical of traditional Australian cooking. The recipes look simple enough, but be warned, it is especially difficult to achieve the light and airy consistency that sets this cake apart from all other cakes.

1 cup plain flour
2 teaspoons baking powder
¾ cup sugar
1 tablespoon melted butter
3 eggs
4 tablespoons milk

1. Place in basin flour and sugar, break in eggs, add melted butter and milk.
2. Beat 3 minutes, then stir in baking powder.
3. Pour into two greased 22 cm cake pans and bake at 190C (375F) for 15 to 20 minutes.

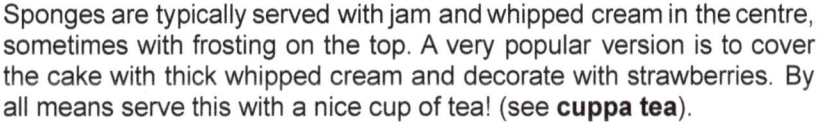

Sponges are typically served with jam and whipped cream in the centre, sometimes with frosting on the top. A very popular version is to cover the cake with thick whipped cream and decorate with strawberries. By all means serve this with a nice cup of tea! (see **cuppa tea**).

About Cooking Sponge (pronounced spunj) **Cake.** There are many stories that purport to explain the failures of cooking sponge cake. We still believe that slamming a door loudly at precisely the wrong moment while the sponge is in the oven will cause it to collapse, or fail to rise. There's no greater embarrassment than to retrieve from the oven, a flat sponge! However, thanks to another Australian favourite, there's something wonderful you can do to camouflage a fallen sponge... you can turn it into lamingtons. Read on!

Lamingtons

Lamingtons are by far the most popular of any Australian cake. They are found at tea parties and social gatherings—especially those of church groups. Lamingtons are that close to being sacred that it doesn't matter! The wonderful thing about lamingtons is that, provided one has the sponge cake, one can produce these classics with hardly any effort.

1 recipe **sponge cake**
chocolate frosting (see **icing**)
desiccated (flaked) coconut

1. Use sponge recipe from above, and pour into well-greased flat pan, so that mixture is approximately 1.5 cm deep.
2. Bake as before.
3. When cake has cooled cut into approximately 2-3 cm squares.
4. Prepare lots of chocolate icing(frosting).
5. Dip each square in chocolate frosting, then sprinkle all over with coconut.

Variation: Instead of chocolate icing, dip squares in strawberry or raspberry Jell-O, and sprinkle with coconut. These are a little more messy, and you should plan on their being eaten right away (which they will be for sure).

About sponge cake in America. Sponge cake does not exist in the USA.. In Australia, one can buy a slab of "golden sponge" which saves having to make the cake. In America slabs of "plain" cake, or angel food cake, almost work, with reasonable results. It's hard to beat the real thing, but even this substitution produces terrific lamingtons. These cakes are named after Lord Lamington, governor of Australia's north eastern state, Queensland, 1895-1901.

Tea Cake

This is a light plain cake, often served with a cup of tea (see **cuppa tea**) in the afternoon.

1½ cups self-rising flour
½ cup sugar
2 tablespoons butter
1 egg
½ cup milk

1. Cream butter and sugar. Add egg, then milk and flour.
2. Pour into well-greased 9 inch cake pan and bake 25 minutes in moderate oven (180C, 360F).
3. While still hot, rub butter on top and sprinkle with cinnamon and sugar.
4. If there is any left the next day, try slices spread with butter, accompanied by a cup of tea, of course.

Authentically Australian? Tea cake is popular in England, where, after all, the tradition of afternoon teas originated.

Date and Apple Tea Cake

60 g. (2 oz.) butter
½ cup sugar
1 egg
1 cup of bran buds
¾ cup of milk
1 ¼ cups self-rising flour
1 pinch salt
1 cup chopped dates
1 grated apple

1. Cream butter and sugar, add egg and beat well.
2. Stir in bran buds, milk, sifted flour and salt, mixing all together lightly.
3. Spread half the mixture in a greased 22.5 cm pan and cover with dates and apple.
4. Spread the remaining cake mixture on top and bake for 30 minutes at 190C (375F).
5. Cover warm cake with lemon icing and sprinkle with chopped dates and nuts.

Banana Tea Cake

60 g. butter
½ cup sugar
1 ½ cups self-rising flour
1 egg
1 banana
½ cup milk
½ teaspoon baking powder

1. Cream butter and sugar, then add egg, milk and flour. Mash banana and mix into ingredients.
2. Bake in moderately hot oven (190C) for 25 minutes.

Orange Cake

2 cups self-rising flour
rind of one orange
2 eggs
½ cup butter
½ cup milk
⅔ cup sugar

1. Beat butter and sugar together, add eggs one at a time, then orange rind. Add milk and flour and beat for one minute.
2. Bake at 204 for ¾ hour. Top with orange frosting (see **icing**)

Lemon Sponge

4 eggs
1 cup sugar
½ cup self-rising flour
1 lemon
juice of half lemon

1. Grate rind of lemon, extract juice.
2. Separate egg whites from yolks. Beat whites stiffly. Addi sugar.
3. Add egg yolks and beat until thick and creamy.
4. Fold in flour, rind and juice.
5. Grease cake pan and place wax paper in bottom.
6. Pour mixture into pan and bake (180C) about 15 minutes.

Apple Cake

½ cup butter
1 ½ cups self rising flour
1 egg
2 teaspoons cocoa
1 teaspoon baking soda, dissolved in 4 teaspoons water

1 cup plain flour
½ cup sugar
1 cup milk
2 teaspoons cinnamon
cup apple sauce

1. Cream butter and sugar, add egg. Sift flour and spices and add gradually, mixing well, alternately with milk.
2. Add apples to which the soda has already been added.
3. Mix in well.
4. Cook in moderate oven (180C (370F) for 40 minutes.
5. Top with chocolate icing (see **icing**). This is a deliciously moist spicy cake.
6. Eat the cake the day you cook it, as it is does not keep well.

White Christmas Cake

125 g. (4 oz.) glacé pineapple
60 g. (2 oz.) glacé figs
60 g. (2 oz.) glacé apricots
½ cup walnuts
2 teaspoons grated lemon rind
¼ cup sweet sherry
1 teaspoon vanilla
1 cup fine sugar

2 ¾ cups plain flour
125 (4 oz.) g. glacé cherries
125 (4 oz.) g. preserved ginger
60 (2 oz.) g. mixed peel
2 tablespoons marmalade
1 teaspoon ground ginger
1 cup butter
2 tablespoons honey
4 eggs

1. Halve cherries and chop remaining fruit and walnuts coarsely.
2. Combine in basin with honey, marmalade, lemon rind, sherry, glycerine and vanilla.
3. Cover and allow to stand overnight.
4. Beat butter until soft, add sugar, beating until light and creamy.
5. Add eggs one at a time making sure to beat well after each egg.
6. Add to fruit mixture, Mix well and stir in sifted dry ingredients.
7. Line a deep cake pan with several layers of wax paper then spread mixture evenly into pan.
8. Bake in very slow oven 120C (300F) for 2½ hours.

Fairy Cakes

Children the world over love miniatures of all kinds. American kids love cup-cakes, standard fare at birthday parties. Not to be outdone, Australian kids have their equivalent, with a little more fanciful name, Fairy Cakes. A generation ago, moms made lots of these, though the practice then was to serve them plain, or perhaps cut open and filled with a little raspberry jam. These days, it's unusual to see them without frosting.

½ cup self-rising flour
½ cup corn flour (corn starch in the U.S.)
2 eggs
vanilla extract
½ cup butter
½ cup sugar

1. Thoroughly mix all ingredients together.
2. Spoon into small muffin pans or into paper patty pans.
3. Bake in moderate oven (180C).

Variation: To make **Butterfly Cakes,** slice top off each cake and cut the slice in half. Top cake with red Jell-O and whipped cream. Insert the two halves of the slice into the topping to make the butterfly wings.

Fudge Cake

1 cup self-rising flour
2 tablespoons cocoa
1 cup crushed cornflakes
½ cup sugar
1 cup coconut
150 g. (4½ oz.) butter
2 tablespoons golden syrup

Melt butter and golden syrup, add to dry ingredients. Press into flat pan and bake about 10 minutes at 190. Top with chocolate icing (see *icing*)

Dream Cake

1½ cups plain flour
1½ teaspoons baking powder (soda)
½ cup of butter
½ cup fine sugar
2 eggs
¼ cup golden syrup
½ cup chopped nuts
Rind of 1 orange
½ cup raisins
½ cup currants
Juice of 1 orange

1. Sift flour and baking soda.
2. Beat butter and little flour together.
3. Separate egg yolks from whites.
4. Beat whites, gradually adding golden syrup.
5. Add yolks, then flour and butter mixture.
6. Beat in baking powder along with remaining flour.
7. Fold in currants, raisins and nuts.
8. Pour into well-greased cake pan.
9. Bake at 175 (350F) for about 1½ hours.

About Golden Syrup. ½ pound brown sugar could be substituted for the golden syrup in this recipe, if you cannot get hold of Golden Syrup at your local store. It will taste OK, but without Golden Syrup you will never know what dream cake really tastes like.

This cake harks back to a time before chocolate was considered a necessity for any cake that could claim the name of Dream Cake. Looks more like a "fruit cake" the legendary cake of eternity.

Candied Fruit Cake Deluxe

180 g. (5 oz.) seeded raisins
2 eggs
125 g. (4 oz.) golden raisins
1 teaspoon baking powder
½ cup brandy
250 g. (8 oz.) whole cherries
½ cup sugar
125 g. (4 oz.) chopped dates
1 cup plain flour
250 g. (8 oz.) glacé apricots
185 g. (6 oz.) stoned prunes
625 g. (¾ lb) whole nuts (brazils, almonds)
250 g. (8 oz.) glacé coarsely chopped pineapple

1. Sift flour and baking powder then sift on to the mixed fruit and toss lightly.
2. Beat the eggs with brandy and sugar until frothy; add to fruit mixture.
3. Mix in nuts until evenly distributed and coated.
4. Grease and line a deep pan and fill.
5. Press down firmly with wetted hands and decorate the top with cherries and nuts.
6. Bake in slow oven (160C, 360F) for 1 ½ hours and cool in pan.
7. While fruit cake addicts prefer their cake "straight" others like the cake topped with a rich glaze:

Apricot Glaze
4 tablespoons strained apricot jam
2 tablespoons sugar
1 tablespoon water

1. Place sugar, water and jam in small pan.
2. Bring slowly to the boil and stir until sugar dissolves.
3. Simmer gently for 2 minutes, then, while cake is still hot, brush liberally with glaze.
4. Leave in pan to cool.

Mango Cheesecake

Cream Cheese Filling
125 g. (4 oz.) cream cheese
½ cup fine sugar
3 medium mangoes, chopped
2 tablespoons gelatin
¼ cup water
1 cup heavy cream

1. Blend cream cheese, sugar and half the mango until smooth.
2. Add cream, blend until combined. Transfer mixture to large bowl.
3. Sprinkle over hot water; cool, but do not allow mixture to set.
4. Add gelatine to mango mixture, stir in remaining mangoes.

Crumb Crust
1 cup plain cookie crumbs (Graham Crackers)
1 cup finely chopped pecans or walnuts
75 g. (3 oz.) butter, melted

1. Combine crumbs, nuts and butter in bowl, mix well.
2. Press evenly over base of greased 9 inch spring-form tin and refrigerate for 30 minutes.
3. Pour filling over cookie base, refrigerate several hours or until set.

Dad's Fruit Cake

250 g. (8 oz.) butter
½ cup brown sugar
2½ cups self-rising flour
4 eggs
1½ teaspoons cinnamon
pinch salt
250 g. (8 oz.) sultanas
250 g. (8 oz.) raisins
250 g. (8 oz.) mixed fruit
½ cup sherry

1. Prepare fruit by mixing mixed fruit, raisins and sultanas, with sherry,
2. Leave to stand. Cream butter and sugar, adding each egg separately.
3. Add flour, cinnamon and beat well in electric mixer.
4. Remove from mixer, and fold in fruit by hand.
5. Grease 20 cm tin and place mixture in tin—mixture will be stiff and heavy to work.
6. Place in oven and bake at 140C (290F) for 2 hours.

About fruit cake in Australia. Fruit cake is, of course, the cake of England, especially popular at Christmas time. It is very popular because it keeps a long time (we have heard of some that has kept for years!). The reason it keeps so long is the sherry, which may be substituted with any fortified wine, or in this recipe 1 tablespoon brandy.

11

Desserts

Australia cannot boast as many authentically Australian desserts as it can cookies and cakes. Some of its puddings are inevitably of English origin. However, their popularity is so strong, and they have been adapted to Australian ingredients in many cases, that it is reasonable to think of them as Australian. This observation applies especially to steamed puddings.

Two desserts deserve special mention, however. These are Pavlova and Peach Melba. They are special because they are named after famous stage performers who toured Australia at the turn of the century. Pavlova was a famous Russian ballet dancer, and Dame Nellie Melba a famous Australian opera singer.

Fruit Jelly ("Jello")

Australian kids call American Jell-O and its equivalents "jelly." There are many variations of this recipe, but one thing is certain: jelly is a perennial kids' favourite.

2 packets Jell-O (different colours)
1½ cups milk
1 tablespoon gelatine
1 tablespoon sugar
3-6 drops vanilla (to taste)
diced fruit

Australia is blessed with a temperate climate, so fresh fruit is abundant. Try to use fresh fruit if you can, but canned fruit (except pineapple) will do (drain before use).

1. Prepare one packet of Jell-O, mixing in diced fruit.
2. Allow to set. Make white jelly by heating milk, almost to a boil, and adding gelatine, sugar and vanilla.
3. Stir until all ingredients are dissolved. Spoon on to fruit Jell-O.
4. Allow to set. Mix second packet of Jell-O, pour on top.
5. Allow to set, cut in squares to serve.

Fruit Salad

This is Australia's most popular summer time dessert. The abundance of fresh fruits ensures that the dish will never fail, and it's so easy to prepare. The serious host would go to the green grocer (a breed making a comeback after being overcome by supermarkets) who is not green but rather specializes in selling all kinds of vegetables and fruits and hand pick all fruits. There are also many local markets these days, and of course, every major city has its big market, such as, for example, the renowned Victoria Market in Melbourne. These might include (but are not limited to) grapes, peaches, pears, apples, oranges, strawberries and bananas. The bananas should be added last and soaked in lemon juice before, to delay browning. Add sugar to taste, though if you have selected your fruits carefully, there should be just enough natural sweetness. Fruit salad is most often served with ice-cream.

Brandied Fruit Salad

400 g. (12 oz.) can red cherries
400 g. (12 oz.) can pineapple pieces
400 g. (12 oz.) can sliced peaches
1 cup sugar
½ cup raisins
½ cup sultanas
1 cup stoned chopped prunes
1 cup brandy

1. Strain juice off canned fruits. Place into an enamel or Pyrex dish.
2. Add sugar, raisins, sultanas and prunes. Bring to boil then simmer for 10 minutes.
3. Add canned fruits and brandy.
4. Place in an airtight jar(s) and leave in the refrigerator for three weeks.
5. Serve with whipped cream or ice-cream. Served at Christmas time in Australia. Other dried fruits such as apricots, can be added, but the variety of colours is an important consideration.

Pavlova

In any season of the year at any party this renowned Australian dessert will be served. A kind of giant meringue, each spoonful of Pavlova instantly dissolves in the mouth. The wonderful thing is that, because Pavlova can be prepared in many different ways, one can always be surprised at a new and delightful variation.

Pavlovas can be difficult to cook unless you know a couple of tricks. Don't have the oven too hot. 135C (280F) is plenty. Don't over-beat the mixture, or the egg whites will toughen, and the Pavlova will shrink too much when cooking. Pavlovas do not keep well. Plan to cook on the day you will serve.

The variations in Pavlovas are achieved mostly by different fillings. The preferred fillings are mounds of whipped cream mixed with fresh fruit in some of the following combinations:
- sliced banana and passion fruit
- fresh raspberries and pineapple
- fresh strawberries and pineapple
- fruit salad

If you're that way inclined, the addition of cordials (called liqueurs in Australia), such as Cointreau, orange curacao or even a little cognac to the appropriate fruits gives the old taste buds an extra kick.

Mum's Pavlova

3-4 egg whites
1 cup fine sugar
1 teaspoon vanilla essence
1 pinch salt
2 tablespoons corn flour (corn-starch)
½ teaspoon cream tartar
1 teaspoon vinegar

1. Beat egg whites until stiff, add sifted dry ingredients, then add vanilla and vinegar.
2. Line a large greased cake pan with wax paper, spoon in mixture.
3. Bake in slow oven (150C, 280F) for 1½ hours.
4. Allow to cool, fill with preferred filling.

Rosemary's Pavlova

This recipe allows you to choose how big you would like to make your Pavlova, using relative quantities.
⅓ cup sugar to each egg white
1 teaspoon corn flour to each egg white

½ teaspoon vinegar to each egg white
egg whites
vanilla

1. Beat eggs until stiff. Add sugar slowly, beating all the time.
2. Fold in corn flour and vinegar. On cookie tray, sprinkle equal parts corn flour and confectioners (castor) sugar.
3. Make a 2-3 inch circular collar of aluminium foil and place on tray. Spoon in mixture.
4. Place in moderate oven (180C, 280F) for half an hour, then reduce heat to 135C (220F) for next hour. Top with favourite filling.

Coffee Pavlova

4 egg whites
1 pinch salt
1½ cups sugar
1 tablespoon corn flour
1 teaspoon instant coffee
1 teaspoon vinegar

1. Place egg whites and salt in clean warm dry bowl and beat until stiff.
2. Gradually beat in half the sugar adding to the mixture a tablespoon at a time, and beating well after each addition.
3. Beat until thick and glossy. Now fold in remaining sugar.
4. Quickly add cornflour, coffee and vinegar.
5. On an upturned 22.5 cm cake pan, sprinkle equal parts corn flour and confectioners' sugar.
6. Tie a band of greased aluminium foil around pan, leaving 7 cm above.
7. Spoon in mixture, bake at 150C (300F) for 1¼ hours.
8. When cold, fill with: ½ pint whipped cream mixed with 1 tablespoon coffee powder, 1 tablespoon Tia Maria or rum (if you must!)
9. Top with grated chocolate.

Lil's Plum (Christmas) Pudding

3 cups plain flour
1 cup sugar
1 cup dark raisins
1 cup currants
2 cups boiling water
1 cup golden raisins
175 g. butter
2 teaspoons baking soda

2 teaspoons allspice
½ teaspoon nutmeg
mixed candied peel
brandy to taste
¼ teaspoon ginger
¼ teaspoon cloves
1 tablespoon cinnamon
3 dates

1. Mix flour, sugar, fruits peel and spices in a bowl.
2. Put boiling water in a saucepan with butter.
3. When boiling add baking soda 1 teaspoon at a time. (Watch carefully, as it may froth over.)
4. Mix the wet with the dry and put into a greased and floured oven-proof bowl.
5. Make a lid of two layers of waxed paper, fasten with string around basin rim.
6. Place in a saucepan and boil 4 hours. Keep level of boiling water about ¾ the way up the pudding.
7. When cool, keep in airtight container in refrigerator.

Plum puddings are best made well ahead of time. They actually improve with age, months even years. To reheat, place in boiling water as before, simmer for 1 hour.

Christmas pudding is usually served with a small sprig of holly inserted in the top of the pudding after it has been placed on a decorative plate. Allow your eager guests to choose from brandy sauce, brandy cream (see **sauces and fillings**) whipped cream or vanilla ice-cream as toppings.

If you're lucky enough to have any left over, sneak down to the kitchen early in the morning on Boxing Day (the day after Christmas), and cut yourself a thin cold slice. Fry it in a little butter, or simply eat it cold with a warm latte. Makes the breakfast of the year!

About Christmas Pudding
Though it might be hot on Christmas day, and some Australians have been known to have Christmas Dinner on the beach, there are few who would allow Christmas to pass without hot Christmas pudding. All Christmas puddings are a variation of what the English call Plum Pudding, although there are no plums in the mixture. Christmas pudding is a special favourite of both old and young. The grown-ups look forward to Christmas Pudding because it is terrific with **brandy sauce**. The kids can hardly contain themselves, because Christmas Pudding is always

served with small coins (silver coins only, which in Australia are 5, 10, and 20 cent pieces, If you decide to try your hand at this fun tradition, make sure you issue several warnings to your excited guests, adults as well as kids. Also, in the olden days when coins were pure silver (or close to it) the coins were cooked right in the pudding. This is no longer a good idea, because the alloys in the coins will leave a nasty taste! Boil the coins separately, then just before serving the pudding, order everyone out of the kitchen, then wedge the coins into the pudding. With a little care, one can hide coins so they cannot be seen too easily—although kids are pretty hard to fool.

Red Caps

Steamed puddings are very English, of course. Not to be outdone, though, Australians have managed to produce a variation on the theme. Red Caps are little steam puddings, cooked in small tea cups, so that each person receives an individual serving.

2 tablespoons butter
½ cup sugar
½ cup self-rising flour
4 tablespoons jam
2 eggs

1. Beat butter and sugar to a cream and add well-beaten eggs and flour.
2. Put jam in four large tea cups (well buttered) and half fill cups with mixture.
3. Place in saucepan in 2 inches of water and steam for half an hour.
4. To serve, tip out on each plate. Great with whipped cream or **custard**.

Pineapple Pudding

Sauce
400 g. (12 oz.) can pineapple rings
¼ cup brown sugar
45 g. (1½ oz.) butter

1. Cream butter and sugar and spread the mixture on the inside of a large greased oven proof dish (22.5 cm).
2. Drain the pineapple rings and place on top of mixture, cutting rings in half if necessary.

Batter
90 g. (3 oz.) butter
2 eggs
½ cup self-rising flour
1 pinch salt
1 tablespoon warm water
½ teaspoon vanilla
⅓ cup fine sugar

1. Cream butter and sugar; add eggs beating well after each addition.
2. Sift flour and salt together and add to mixture along with water and vanilla.
3. Spread batter over top of pineapple.
4. Bake in moderate oven (180C, 350F) 35 to 40 minutes.
5. Turn pudding upside down on serving dish, so that pineapple sits on top of batter.

This dish is delicious served warm with ice-cream. If there's any leftover (not likely) you can use it the next day as a cake. It cuts nicely into slices. Try it with a nice cup of tea (see **cuppa tea**) especially if you drink tea without sugar.

About pineapple. Pineapple was not often found in Australian recipes prior to the 1960s, even though it was widely cultivated in Queensland, Australia's tropical north eastern state, for many decades. Today, pineapple more than any other fruit sets Australian dishes apart from their English cooking heritage. Pineapple is most typical in Australian meat dishes (see **casseroles**).

Golden Pudding

60 g. (2 oz.) butter
½ teaspoon baking soda
1 cup self-rising flour
1 pinch salt
¾ cup of milk
4 tablespoons golden syrup

1. Melt butter in pan and add syrup, milk and baking soda, salt and the sifted flour. Mix well together.
2. Pour into greased pudding basin and cover with aluminium foil. Place in pan of water, and boil for 2 hours.

As we have noted elsewhere Golden Syrup is a popular cooking ingredient in many Australian desserts. Substitutes are difficult. For this recipe you could try using the same quantity of marmalade, since there are quite a few other golden pudding recipes that exclusively use it instead of golden syrup. It is likely that marmalade is the authentic English version of this popular pudding, and Golden Syrup is the Australian adaptation.

Mum's Pineapple Dessert

400 g. (12 oz.) can pineapple
1 packet raspberry Jell-O
2 eggs
1 litre milk
a little sugar

3. Drain juice from pineapple, cut small and place in glass dish.
4. Make a custard from egg yolk, sugar and milk, pour over pineapple,
5. Place in refrigerator and allow to set.
6. Make jelly from pineapple juice and Jell-O.
7. When setting, beat egg whites stiffly and fold into Jell-O.
8. Spread over custard and allow to set.
9. Serve with whipped cream.

Hope's Sweet

1 can (380 ml) unsweetened condensed milk (chilled)
⅓ cup fine sugar
milk (chilled)
2 teaspoons gelatine
2 tablespoons coffee essence or..
2 tablespoons coffee cordial or..
pulp of 4 passion fruit

1. Pour unsweetened milk into bowl and beat. Add fine sugar.
2. Dissolve gelatine in ½ cup boiling water and add to mixture when cool.
3. Add your choice of coffee or passion fruit.
4. Place in refrigerator and chill.
5. Serve with chocolate mint wafers.

About coffee essence. Coffee essence has a distinctive taste, not especially like coffee as we know it today. In olden days, coffee essence was always sold mixed with chicory, which is what gave it the different taste.

Peach Trifle

400 g. (12 oz.) can peaches
1¼ cups custard
½ cup peach juice
½ teaspoon gelatine
1 egg white
1 recipe **sponge cake**
lemon butter

1. Drain peaches and save juice, spread pieces of sponge with lemon butter (see **fillings**).
2. Place sponge cake in dish then sliced peaches and cover with custard.
3. Dissolve gelatine in heated peach juice and when nearly set beat into a stiffly beaten egg white.
4. Spoon on top and decorate with peaches and nuts.
5. **Variation:** Soak pieces of sponge in sherry.

Peach Melba

This popular Australian dessert is made up in individual glass dishes. For each serving you will need:
1 piece of **sponge cake**
1 half large peach (fresh or canned)
peach syrup
sweet sherry (sprinkling only!)
whipped cream
pureed strawberries and/or raspberries

1. Place the sponge in bottom of glass dish, top with half peach, cut side up. Sprinkle with peach syrup and sweet sherry.
2. Pipe large mound of whipped cream into centre of peach.
3. Pour strawberries and raspberries over peach and sponge.
4. If preferred, place scoop of vanilla ice-cream in centre of each peach before adding cream.

About Melba. This dessert was named after the great opera singer Dame Nellie Melba, or at least, so the story goes. It is popular in many Australian restaurants, and appears constantly in many different variations. Dame Nellie Melba was a legend in her own time. Just the sound of her name—a contraction of Melbourne, her birth place—sent people into swoons of adoration. Dame Nellie rose to success at the Royal Covent Garden in London during the golden years of opera, and dominated the international scene from the 1890s till well after World War I. In 1914, she played one performance at Covent Garden before no fewer than seven kings and queens. In San Francisco in 1898, her rendition of The Star Spangled Banner in the music lesson scene of the Barber of Seville to a despondent audience at the height of the Spanish American war, brought the house down. On her international tours especially to Australia, she was mobbed by screaming crowds in much the same way that rock stars are mobbed today. She accepted this as her due, noting, "There are lots of Duchesses, but only one Melba."

Apple Pancakes

1-2 apples
½ cup plain flour
1 pinch salt
1 egg
1¼ cups milk
1 lemon
30 g. butter

1. Sift flour and salt, break egg into the mound of flour.
2. Using a wooden spoon, gradually stir flour into the egg until it will take no more.
3. Add half the milk gradually, until all flour is absorbed.
4. Beat well until bubbles form. (If batter is well beaten, the pancakes will be lighter.)
5. Stir in the rest of the milk, and allow to stand for 1 hour.
6. Peel and grate apples, fold into mixture.
7. So that your pancakes will be thin, make mixture a little thinner than would be usual for American Pancakes.
8. Place a small piece of butter in the pan, melt, then pour out and wipe out with paper towel.
9. Place another piece of butter in pan, and heat till quite hot.
10. Drop large spoonful of batter into pan and fry until golden brown; turn with wide knife or slice.
11. When cooked on both sides, remove and place on piece of paper. Sprinkle with confectioners' sugar.

These pancakes should be thin and large in size, so that they can be rolled up, and served on a hot plate. Serve with additional sugar plus a slice of lemon. They are delicious with lemon juice and sugar. Whipped cream is a bit of all right too!

About pancakes. It's hard to imagine how Australia could have anything new to offer America, the land of pancakes. One never sees apple pancakes like these in any American restaurant. Apple fritters—slices of apple deep fried in batter—are common enough, but they are unequal to the delicacy of flavour and texture of these apple pancakes.

Pikelets (Drop Scones)

These are a variation of pancakes, but are smaller, thicker and a little heavier than the usual pancake.

½ cup self-rising flour
1 pinch salt
4 tablespoons fine sugar
1 egg
⅓-½ cup milk

1. Sift flour and salt, add sugar.
2. Drop unbeaten egg into middle of bowl and stir.
3. Add enough milk until the batter is fairly thick.
4. Beat well. Have griddle hot and well oiled (not margarine, use cooking oil), but not too much oil as uneven browning may result.
5. Drop a spoonful of the batter onto the griddle (use a tablespoon).
6. Turn once only.
7. Serve on hot plate.

Offer a variety of jellies, butter, jam, honey and whipped cream for toppings. In America, of course, one would naturally use maple syrup. This syrup is not widely available in Australia, because the climate is not conducive to maple trees—not enough rain and too warm a climate. These days, though, imitation maple syrup is widely available. Once upon a time Aussies did not eat pancakes for breakfast, as have Americans for as long as one can remember. Today, anything goes, especially for brunch, where Aussies enjoy pancakes, banana, bacon and syrup.

11

Icing, Fillings and Spreads

Australian icing has a different consistency from the frosting most commonly found on American cakes and cookies. It is not as soft, and develops a slightly hard surface when it dries. There is a type of icing used on decorative cakes, such as wedding cakes, which Australians call "plastic icing." This icing is very thick and sweet, often flavoured with almond essence. As its name implies, it isn't really meant to be eaten, only for decoration. Lemon spreads and fillings are popular, along with various sauces that are used on Christmas puddings. Brandy cream is one such sauce.

Brandy Cream

1 egg
¾ cup sugar
½-1 cup whipped cream
3 tablespoons brandy

1. Beat white of egg until stiff; gradually add fine sugar.
2. Beat egg yolk slightly and add whipped cream.
3. Fold into egg and sugar mixture.
4. For thicker sauce, add more whipped cream. Pour in brandy slowly.
5. When plum pudding is served piping hot, pour sauce over each serving.

Vanilla Icing (Frosting)

1 cup sugar
1 white of egg
½ cup of water
1-2 drops vanilla, if required

1. Boil water and sugar together until a thread forms from a fork dipped into the mixture.
2. Beat the white of egg until stiff.
3. Allow mixture to slightly cool, then pour over egg, add vanilla if preferred, and beat until a thick cream forms. Spread over cake.

Chocolate Icing

½ cup confectioners' sugar
4 tablespoons grated chocolate
    or
2 tablespoons cocoa
3 tablespoons water

1. Sift sugar and place in saucepan with chocolate or cocoa.
2. Add water and stir until warm. Spread over cake.

Lemon Icing

1 cup sugar
1 lemon

1. Place sugar and juice of lemon in saucepan.
2. Stir until all lumps are gone and thick cream has formed.
3. Spread over cake.

Passion Fruit Spread

Passion fruits are extremely popular in Australia, whether used in spreads, jellies or in Pavlova (see **Pavlova**) fillings. Passion fruit grow on a vine, which may be cultivated similar to a grape vine (although the leaves and stems are very different from grape vines). The fruit is about the size and shape of an egg, with a smooth skin, a deep brownish purple in colour, like the colour of eggplant. When thoroughly ripe, the skin shrivels and becomes very wrinkled. This is a sign that the inside is sweet and delicious. The fruit inside is a bright yellow pulp containing scores of small black seeds.

Australians eat the seeds as well as the pulp, even though *The Joy of Cooking* recommends against it. Just pour the pulp on vanilla ice-cream for a tasty treat. And the spread goes well in sandwiches, buttered of course..

3 eggs
60 g. (2 oz.) butter
8 passion fruits
2 cups sugar
8 tablespoons lemon juice
8 tablespoons water

Beat eggs, add rest of ingredients and mix together. Simmer until thick. Allow to cool, store in refrigerator in closed container. Spread thinly on bread and butter.

Mocha Fondue Sauce

250 g..(8 oz.) milk chocolate
2 tablespoons instant coffee powder
¾ cup of thickened cream
2 tablespoons cordial (Tia Maria)

1. Break chocolate into small pieces. Place into a heavy based pan with the cream and instant coffee.
2. Stir over gentle heat until chocolate is melted.
3. Add cordial and serve in a heat proof dish.
4. Serve with pieces of fruit, strawberries, banana or pineapple and cubes of cake.
5. Whipped cream may be served also. Guests dip pieces of fruit into the sauce and eat.

Betsy's Lemon Filling

1 cup sugar
1 cup water
2 lemons for juice
1-2 teaspoons grated lemon rind
2 tablespoons corn flour
2 tablespoons custard powder
1 tablespoon butter
Boil sugar, water, juice and rind together.

1. Thicken with corn flour and custard powder, adding butter when thickened. Will set when cool.
2. **Hint**: Use less sugar if lemons are not so sour or if you like your filling sharp.

Lemon Butter

1 lemon
1 cup sugar
60 g. (2 oz.)butter
2 eggs

1. Grate rind from lemon, extract juice.
2. Soften butter, mix with sugar and rind.
3. Add lemon juice until desired consistency.

12

Drinks and Drinking

Australia is a society of drinkers, of which there are two classes: tea drinkers and beer drinkers (and more recently wine drinkers, but that's another story). Who drinks what depends on the time of the day and the day of the week. The day is divided according to when one drinks, and what one drinks. Cups of tea help break up the day's work. Glasses of beer help one relax after a day's work, and pass the time on Saturdays. In the old days, there was no beer on Sundays. You had to take home your bottles of beer the night before. These days, pubs are open Sundays in many places, although they are less frequented on those days, except by the younger set. Sundays are more for visiting friends and relatives and drinking tea.

There are certain unwritten rules about how to fix drinks (both beer and tea) and how to behave socially when drinking. Drinking beer before lunch time on a weekday or before about 11.00 a.m. on a Saturday is considered to be a sign of an "alky" (alcoholic). The exception to this rule is when you are on a weekend binge with the mates (perhaps a footy or fishing trip) during which time it might be a sign of drinking strength to have a beer for breakfast. Tea can be taken at any hour.

Beer and tea are enjoyed especially at spectator sports, such as Aussie rules football (footy) and cricket. Actually, cricket would be dead without either. Traditionally, the great "Test matches" take five days to finish. Today, though, there are many one day matches, so the boring wait for action is cut down quite a bit Nevertheless, spectators may take to playing cards and drinking large quantities of beer to fill in the time between each moment of excitement when a batsman is bowled out or hits a six (a home run). The highlights of cricket are the breaks for tea every afternoon, and the strange names for field positions (such as "silly mid on," "slips" and "square leg").

The situation with Aussie rules footy is a little different. This game, is played on a huge oval shaped field, about twice the size of an American football field, with 18 players on each side. Many spectators take along their flask of tea to sip and keep warm. Although most stadiums now have lots of seating, in bygone days thousands of fans stood for the entire game (four quarters of around 30 minutes each) just as they would probably stand in the bar after the game. Beer helps to lubricate the voices of the barrackers (spectators who yell), many of whom spend much time heaping abuse on the umpire (referee). When there is a lot of beer, blues (brawls) break out among the yahoos (rowdy hooligans) and drongoes ("bloody no-hopers"). Things got so bad over the years, that most footy stadiums will not allow spectators to bring their own beer into the stadium (they used to bring in car fridges full of them). Now, one can only buy beer at the stadium, and never in bottles —this is because the bottles hurt the players and umpire when thrown at them. There are also, now, non-drinking sections of the stadiums.

Soda is just as popular as in America. But if you ask for a soda in a milk bar (see below) you will not be understood, or will be given soda water, and thought to be weird. You have to ask for "soft drink" or ask for a specific flavour. There is a wider range of soda flavours available in Australia compared with the U.S., including some that are hardly known in America, such as passion fruit. (Though some exotic flavours have begun to appear in certain fruit juices and iced teas). Aussie kids drink a lot of "cordial" which is sweet, non-carbonated drink that is mixed up from a concentrate and tastes something like Gatorade. Flavours available are usually various citrus and tropical fruits.

Also once popular was a powder called, variously, "lemon saline" which most Moms kept in their kitchens. This tastes not unlike some popular brands of digestive carbonated ("fizzy") drinks, such as *Brioschi*, but with a stronger lemon flavour. Saline is thought to be a very good thirst quencher. These days, though, Aussie drinks are not distinguishable from their American counterparts, with power drinks, sports drinks, organic drinks, you name it.

Two other "cordials" (these are not alcoholic and are nothing like American cordials, which are called liqueurs in Australia) are worthy of mention. These are lemon squash and lime juice cordial. One occasionally sees these at an American gourmet food store, and even in a regular supermarket. A little lime juice cordial mixed with cold soda water is a wonderful thirst quencher on a hot day, of which Australia has many. Lemon squash cordial is mixed with soda water to make a drink called lemon squash. One buys these mainly in a bar. They are almost acceptable in lieu of drinking beer (almost).

Many countries have distinctive settings where people traditionally meet to drink a little and talk. Australia has two such abodes. A Pub is the most widely established place to go if you wish to speak with "the locals" and drink beer. In the old days, if you wanted to drink anything else, you were probably better off not going to a bar, but these days things are a lot different, except, perhaps in the more remote country pubs. All pubs now serve coffee (even cappuccino!) and many non-alcoholic drinks. While the number of pubs has probably declined in the past couple of decades, one is constantly amazed at the number of pubs in every Australian town. There is certainly no shortage of them. Pubs are essentially meeting places to talk, joke, sometimes play darts or snooker, but certainly never for business. You might be able to place a few bets on the horses as well, not to mention, in some localities play the pokies (poker machines).

Another Australian institution is the Milk Bar, though slowly disappearing. These little corner stores are everywhere in the suburbs and towns. If you like milk drinks, especially milk shakes, then these are the places to go. You will have to stand up, though, while you drink your milk shake. Milk Bars tend to be very small, and have no space for seating. Kids go to them mostly, usually on errands for Mum to buy a few small cooking items like butter or sugar; or to buy some lollies (candy) with small change.

In contrast to beer drinking, tea drinking has not until very recently taken place in public places. Tea rooms are in ample supply in England (as are Pubs), where one can get a good cup of tea, and a scone or biscuits. There have never been as many tea rooms in Australia as in England, and many of those that existed have become coffee shops that boast cappuccino and espresso coffee. But that is another story, and another cookbook! Our guess is that the tea room did not flourish in Australia for the simple reason that people of our parents' generation did not trust others to make a good cup of tea. Tea was a drink made only at home. Only there could one be sure that it would be made according to one's taste. So, how to make a good cuppa?

Cuppa Tea (Cup of Tea)

Items and ingredients required are:
Medium sized teapot (preferably china)
tea cosy
sugar to taste
English breakfast tea
boiling water
tea cups and saucers
teaspoons
whole milk to taste
tea strainer (optional)

1. Boil water using any . Pour a little boiling water into tea pot and swirl around so that the tea pot becomes warm. This is very important (not sure why, but it is).
2. Measure out the amount of tea you will need. One level teaspoon per cup is the usual guide, then add "one for the pot."
3. Immediately pour the rapidly boiling water into the pot. Replace lid, cover with a tea cosy to keep it warm. A tea cosy is usually a knitted thing that slips over the tea pot like a ski mask. It is often an ancient family heirloom that some distant aunt knitted. Do not place tea pot over heat at this stage (or any stage for that matter), or bring to boil. This will ruin the taste of the tea (makes it taste like dish water).
4. The tea must now be left to "draw" for a while. This will normally take about 5 minutes or more. Some hasten this process by lifting the tea pot and gently tilting it back and forth. It's better simply to wait. There are other things to do, anyway.
5. While the tea is drawing, ask your tea drinkers how they take their tea. In Australia, to respond to this question that you will have yours black with lemon, while tolerated, would not be considered well. Only on special occasions do Aussies drink their tea with lemon. People do drink tea black, but most drink it white.
6. Now we come to the sticky part. It is rumoured that the Queen (of England, of course) adds the milk to her tea last. The established practice in Australia is the opposite. The milk must be placed in the cup first. The tea tastes much better this way, although you have to be more adept at guessing the amount of milk to pour in the cup, especially as you can be rarely sure how strong the tea will be when it is poured. A rule of thumb is to pour about half an inch of milk into the cup. While it would be best if you didn't, it's OK to ask a guest whether the tea is strong enough, and to add either tea, milk, or more hot water, to adjust to the desired strength.
7. Having resolved this problem to your satisfaction, place the strainer on the cup and pour the tea through it. Always pour the tea in the kitchen, then take the cup to your guest. Never allow any tea to

splash into the saucer. (This seems a bit silly, since surely this is exactly what the saucer is for!). An alternative is to pass around the cups, then bring the tea pot and small pitcher of milk around, and allow guests to pour their own. In this case, though, one must have a silver tea service —an ornate silver tea pot with small silver milk jug covered with a doily with little beads sewn into its edge.

8. Depending on how strong the tea pours, fill the cup to about 1 cm from the top. If the tea strength seems all right (it should be a soft tan colour), top the cup up to about 4 mm from the top with boiling water.

9. Tea drinkers always add their own sugar if they wish.

10. A tea strainer is certainly desirable, because it makes drinking the last half inch of the tea from the cup much easier. However, there is no special rule about this. If you do not use a strainer, and your guest takes a second cup of tea, always empty out the dregs of tea leaves from the cup first, before refilling.

11. After you have poured the first cups of tea, refill the tea pot with more boiling water, and allow to draw once again, while you drink your first cups.

12. Don't use fancy teas, rose tea, mint tea, Chinese tea, or whatever. They may be fine for other purposes, but for making a true blue Aussie cuppa, there's no place for them here.

Beer (and Beer Drinking)

Making "home brew" is as popular in Australia as it is in England and America. The recipes are much the same, so we will not reproduce them here. However, with a little knowledge of the drinking customs of Aussies, one may approximate certain beer-related drinks using ingredients available in the United States.

Beer and Stout
Australian beers, and beers from just about everywhere can be bought from most American beverage stores these days. Fosters is the most widely distributed Australian beer in America. One can find those huge cans of Fosters and regular sized bottles in most places. Coopers beer (from South Australia) is also available from time to time. This beer is the closest one can get to a commercialized home brew. It has a sediment in the bottom (it's supposed to), so if that puts you off, leave the bottle sit for a day or so before you drink it. And when you pour, pour slowly so that air does not bubble back into the bottle and disturb the sediment. Leave about the last ¼ inch of sediment in the bottle. Of course, some prefer the sediment to be left in and mixed into the rest of the bottle of beer. These days, with micro-breweries everywhere, cloudy beer, especially wheat beer, is viewed as a good thing.

Australian stout (Coopers makes some) is rarely found in American stores. However, the classic Irish stout, Guinness is available everywhere. While stout and beer are great on their own, one can make popular Australian drinks by mixing them.

Mother-In-Law ("Black and Tan," "Half and Half")
In a 220 ml (10 oz.) glass, pour stout up to within 2.5 cm of the rim. Top up with a bitter beer, that is, not an ale or lager, but a beer. (Canada makes lots of these.) What's in the name? The drink is "stout and bloody bitter."

Shandy
If you ask for a lemonade in Australia, you will be given a soda that looks and tastes very much like Seven Up. A Shandy is made by pouring beer to within 1-3 cm of the top of the glass, then topping up with lemonade. Children are commonly allowed to drink a light shandy (lemonade with a dash of beer) on special occasions. Try it. Some like it, some hate it.

Beer Culture
By the way, Aussies have quite a disarming sense of humour which can catch Americans unawares. The favourite pastime is to kid or rubbish mates (not usually done to strangers, unless there's good reason for it). This can amount to quite personal remarks about how one does just about everything (or how one can't do things), and appears to the outsider as insulting and uncouth. The extent to which one can take this

good-natured ribbing shows how good a "bloke" (genuine fellow) one is. In a bar, Australians will also spin yarns (tell tall tales), especially to unsuspecting visitors from another country. Again, this is part of the Aussie sense of humour, and should not be taken personally. Aussies are great kidders!

Aussie beer drinkers take their beer drinking very seriously, as they do their tea drinking. Beer must be poured just right, and in the right glass. There was an outcry quite some years back new health regulations required that fresh clean glasses be provided each time the customer in a bar ordered a beer. This regulation cut across the time honoured and much studied practice of always using the same glass for a refill.

The reason for the outcry was that an experienced beer drinker can tell one glass of beer from another, even though to the uninitiated they may look the same. A fresh glass usually does not retain the head (white froth at the top) as well as a used glass. This is extremely important for Aussie beer drinkers. If you pour them a glass of beer that has no "head," it will be returned to you with a comment like, "I don't drink dog's ... " Or, "What do yer think I am, a *** Pom (Englishman)?"

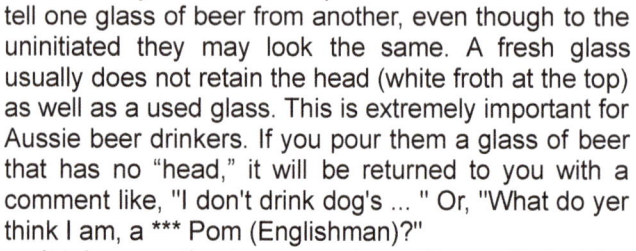

It takes practice to pour a glass of beer with just the right amount of head (froth). In Victoria, about 1 cm of froth is considered right. Too much froth is also unacceptable:. If you serve a beer with a lot of froth, an Aussie might remark, "Well, yer gunna put a bow-tie on it, mate?" At home an Aussie beer drinker will also have experimented with different detergents, to find out which ones produce the best beer glasses. Many wash their beer glasses separately from other dishes without any detergent at all, because it is thought that detergent ruins the head-keeping capabilities of the glass. Many hours may be passed in a bar discussing the science of beer pouring.

Drinking Beer in bygone days.

Things have changed. Now, it's common to see women in the "public bar." In bygone days, here were the rules:

1. Women were not welcome in a public bar in a classic Aussie Pub. There was no law against it (though there used to be!). The woman's place was the "Ladies Lounge" or "Saloon Bar" where the surroundings and clientele would be more designed for sheilas (girls). Though one still gets the feel of male exclusivity in some out of the way country pubs, by and large the public bar as a men's haven is gone.
2. To soften the shock of entering into a Public Bar, the Saloon Bar was common where the ambience was a little quieter and one paid a little more for the beer. Also, one could order mixed drinks without being made fun of (mostly). These days. The pokies (poker machines) have encroached on every spare inch of the pub, so saloon bars have in many cases morphed into gaming parlours.
3. Drinking schools. Not the kind with desks and teachers. Rather, the kind that fish congregate in. A "drinking school" (a group of three or more drinkers) requires that each member of the school "shout" (take his turn in paying for a round of drinks). Anyone who pulls out in the middle of a round, or who doesn't take his turn, is considered to be a bludger (free loader). Obviously, if the school is large, you're in for quite a time. The only way to extricate oneself from such a situation is to pay for an extra round of drinks before you leave.
4. *Bar stools.* Be careful which stool you sit on. Very often there are set places where the local boozers (steady drinkers) always sit.

Aussie pubs have changed a lot. Though they are still rowdy places on Friday and Saturday nights, (but no longer smoke-filled) and smelling of yeast and beer soaked into the very woodwork of the buildings, they are also congenial places, where one can always find a mate to talk to.

The tradition of heavy beer drinking probably dates back to shearing times late in the 19th century. The shearers would work constantly until the shearing was done, receiving meals and lodging on the homestead. When the shearing was completed the men would be paid their checks. Many took off to the nearest pub in search of relaxation and excitement. To be "lambed down" was to be led astray by others, or oneself, into spending an entire check on booze:

> The shades of night were falling fast,
> As down a steep gully passed
> A man whom you could plainly see
> Had just come off a drunken spree,
> Lambed down.
> He'd left the station with his check,
> And little evil did he wreck;

> At Ryan's pub he felt all right,
> And yet he was, before next night,
> Lambed down.
> 'Oh, stay! old Ryan said, 'and slip
> Your blanket off, and have a nip;
> I'll cash your check and send you on.'
> He stopped, and now his money's gone-
> Lambed down.
> He's got the shakes and thinks he sees
> Blue devils lurking in the trees;
> Oh, shearers! if you've any sense
> Don't be on such pretence
> Lambed down.

-- *Lambed Down*, Anonymous, about 1870.

Why devote so much space to beer drinking? Fact is, alcohol has played an important part in Australia's history.

Rum was the main form of currency in early Colonial days. It was dear to the hearts of all Aussies:

> *Convicts' Rum Song*
> Cut yer name across me backbone,
> Stretch me skin across a drum
> Iron me up on Pinchgut Island
> From today till Kingdom Come!
> I will eat yer Norfolk Dumpling
> Like a juicy Spanish plum,
> Even dance the Newgate Hornpipe*
> If ye'll only give me RUM!
> —Anonymous

13

Outback Cooking

America has her Wild West. Australia has her Outback. Many of Australia's most moving novels are set in the Outback. There lies the mystery and romance of Australia. The outback is enormous, about four fifths of the country's area. There is also a lot of bush land in the high plains surrounding the coastal areas, teaming with wild life. In the North East, where the climate is tropical, there is abundant wild life and vegetation. With such a varied climate, there is a wide range of plants and animals, many of which are edible. Australia's indigenous peoples lived off this land for many centuries. Only recently have Australians begun to learn about and experiment with such truly Australian foods.

One would have thought that the early settlers, stuck in the isolation of the Outback, would have to "live off the land." But the fact is that Australia's early settlers brought their traditional foods with them—flour, tea, beef, lamb (and rabbits!)—the traditional foods of their Anglo-Saxon culture. But traditional Outback cooking draws on the romance of Outback wilderness that emphasizes the primitive use of the camp fire as the vehicle of cooking anything.

Also included are recipes that could not be easily reproduced in the Australian outback without the help of gourmet food stores and a modern kitchen. In recent years there has been a strong movement in Australia to find a cuisine that is "uniquely Australian" which is to say, a cuisine that uses ingredients of Australia's indigenous flora and fauna. Some of these ingredients one might find by foraging in the forests, but most of them could only be found by an expert in such matters. They can more likely be found in gourmet food stores or Australian souvenir shops. One may experience them in a restaurant that serves "modern Australian" cuisine, although "modern Australian" usually also includes the many adaptations of Asian and other imported cultural influences on Australian cooking of the past 20 years or so. The hunters among you may find substitutions easier to accomplish than others.

About Outback Cooking

There is greater opportunity to try out bush cooking in many parts of the United States because the danger of forest fires is not so great (depending, of course, on where one lives in the States). If you do try some Outback cooking, please, please use fire safety. Don't have a large fire, just a very small one is needed for most cooking, and clear the ground for 10 feet (3 mt) around. Preferably, use the safest type of cooking fire, a trench fire. All one needs is a small trench dug in the ground, with the fire lit in the trench. In most of Australia during the summer months, it would be extremely unlikely that one could light a cooking fire in the bush, due to the danger of fire (and there are severe punishments for doing so). Most Aussies, during these months, if they do want to cook outdoors, will use a portable gas barbecue. But there are even many days of extreme fire danger when gas barbecues cannot be used. In public parks, electric barbecues are provided, often free.

The best time to cook in the Australian bush is in the late winter or early spring. The smell of eucalyptus just after it has rained is hard to beat. Better than the smell of a pine forest, though this is a little bit like comparing rubies and diamonds. By the way, Australians call eucalyptus trees "gum trees." There are about 1,000 varieties, of which the famed koala eats only one.

About killing and eating Australian wild life.
Killing animals in order to eat, if one is actually dependent on the land for survival, seems surely reasonable. But we doubt that there is anyone who actually does this in Australia today, including the indigenous peoples, although some few in the far North of Australia may continue to try to cling to the old ways. Recipes are included that require you to have in hand a dead animal or two. Frankly, they're included for the sake of curiosity. One wouldn't want to see a single hair (or scale) of any Australian animal harmed.

Lately the farming of certain species has become popular, so that their meat is now available in upscale restaurants under the guise of exotic sounding dishes. There are now farms for emu (the large flightless bird similar to the ostrich), crocodiles, camels (imported early in the 19th century to help transportation in Australia's desert), buffalo (water buffalo, a different species from the American), and kangaroo. In some parts of Australia where kangaroos are abundant, it is permitted to hunt them (only certain species). Many fish are also farmed such as oysters, barramundi, and even yabbies (fresh water crayfish or lobster).

Roast Tasmanian Hen

This recipe is unique in its use of vine leaves. Grapes were introduced into Australia from California. The Tasmanian hen, (not the native hen though) locally called "bantam," is very popular. There are other hens or fowl, such as the Mallee fowl, scrub hen, bush turkey (about the size of a small hen) and the Australian water hen. American substitution: quail or Cornish game hen.

Tasmanian hens, Quail, or Cornish Hen

1 slice bacon per bird
Vine leaves
30 g. (1 oz.) melted butter
Fried bread
Red currant jelly
Dried bread crumbs

1. Truss each hen and brush with melted butter.
2. Place vine leaf on the breast and bacon slice on top. Secure with strong toothpick or skewer.
3. Cover lightly with aluminium foil and roast for 30 minutes at 200C (400F).
4. Baste frequently.
5. To fry bread, heat oil to very hot temperature (as for French fries) and drop in squares of day-old bread.
6. Quickly brown and remove so that it remains crisp.
7. Serve hen on fried bread spread with red currant jelly.
8. Top with gravy sprinkled with dried bread crumbs.

Wallaby Stew

Wallabies are small kangaroos. As with wild rabbit, wallaby and kangaroo meat are very lean.

750 g. (1½ lb.) wallaby meat
500 g. (16 oz.) can pineapple pieces (save juice)
2 onions. sliced
120 g. (4 oz.) bacon (optional)
½ cup tomato juice
½ cup beef bouillon
1 tablespoon parsley, chopped
Salt and pepper
¼ teaspoon dried basil
¼ cup flour

1. If bacon is used, make it is as lean as possible.
2. Mix basil with flour. Cut meat into one-inch pieces and roll in flour and basil.
3. Place half of meat in bottom of well-greased casserole dish and cover with half of the bacon, parsley, onion and pineapple pieces.
4. Add salt and pepper to taste. Repeat layers until no ingredients are left.
5. Combine ¼ cup of pineapple juice, bouillon and tomato juice and pour over casserole. Bake, covered, for about two hours at 175C (350F).

The wallaby has a special place in the hearts of all Aussies, perhaps because in olden days, kangaroos and wallabies were the guarantee to the poor that there was always a meal there, waiting to be caught, even in the most trying times, as expressed in the following ballad, *Stir the Wallaby Stew:*

> Poor Dad he got five years or more as everybody knows,
> And now he lives in Maitland Jail with broad arrows on his clothes,
> He branded all of Brown's clean-skins and never left a tail,
> So I'll relate the family's woes since Dad got put in jail.
> Chorus
> So stir the wallaby stew,
> Make soup of the kangaroo tail,
> I tell you things is pretty tough
> Since Dad got put in jail.
> They let Dad out before his time, to give us a surprise.
> He came and slowly looked around and gently blessed our eyes,

He shook hands with the shearer cove and said he thought things stale,
So left things here to shepherd us and battled back to jail.

--Anonymous, mid 1800s.

A Wallaby is a small species of kangaroo. American substitution for wallaby could be possum or squirrel. There are also possums in Australia, but we don't know of any tradition of eating them. Besides, they're a protected species (not like in New Zealand).

Pan-fried Kangaroo Steak in Port Wine Sauce

1 kg (2 lb.) of kangaroo steak, best cut
4 tablespoons butter
salt and pepper

Port Wine Sauce
½ cup of water
Grated rind and juice of 3 small oranges
2 tablespoons margarine
3 tablespoons corn flour
2 tablespoons sugar
Freshly ground black pepper
¼ cup of port wine

1. Cut steak into thin slices. Sprinkle with salt and black pepper.
2. Fry in butter until a rich brown on both sides.
3. Remove from pan. Simmer orange rind in water for 5 minutes, strain and add liquid to juice or oranges.
4. Make up to one cup with extra water, if necessary.
5. Add margarine to pan and heat, stirring in corn flour (about 2 minutes).
6. Gradually blend in orange liquid and cook slowly until thickened.
7. Return kangaroo steak to pan and add sugar, pepper and port.
8. Simmer for two minutes or until tender.
9. *Be careful not to overcook or the meat will become very tough.* Adjust amount of liquid by adding water or port to taste.

This recipe is for the large "buck" kangaroos that grow to over 4 m. tall. American substitution for kangaroo steak: young venison.

Roast Wild Pig with Minted Apricots

Care must be taken in preparation of this game animal. Make sure that it is well cooked. American substitution: peccary.

1 wild pig carefully cleaned and washed
½ lemon
1 medium can apricot halves, drained
90 g. (3 oz.) cottage cheese
4 tablespoons mint, finely chopped
Salt and pepper

1. Preheat oven to 200C (400F). Rub pig with lemon half and place in roasting dish. Allow 35 minutes per 500 g., (1 lb.) plus an additional 35 minutes, for cooking time.
2. Combine cottage cheese, mint, salt and pepper.
3. Fill apricot halves. Place in shallow pan and bake in over 15 minutes before serving.
4. Decorate pig by attaching apricot halves to outside of pig with toothpick An occasional maraschino cherry will add to the visual effect.

Roast Wild Duck, Victorian Style

Stuffing:
3 medium onions
1 tablespoon sage, finely chopped
250 g. (½ lb.) bread crumbs
30 g. (1 oz.) butter
1 egg
Salt and pepper to taste

1. Prepare and truss duck as for any game bird.
2. Stuff body with sage/onion stuffing.
3. Roast at 200C (400F) for about 1½ hours or more, according to age.
4. Serve with roast tomatoes, baked apples and roast potatoes.

About Australian Ducks. The Australian grey or black duck is hunted in most of Australia where there is sufficient habitat. . This recipe originated from Australia's south eastern state of Victoria.

Murray Roll

Pastry:
Any ready-made pastry will do. Puff pastry is sometimes used, though depending on the herbs used, puff pastry may make this dish a little too rich.

Fish:
4 large Murray Cod fillets, rolled in flour and sprinkled with salt and pepper to taste.

Sauce:
30 g. (1 oz.) butter or margarine
Up to 60 g. (2 oz.) plain flour
½ cup milk
½ cup cooked peas
½ cup water (use water from cooked peas)
1 tablespoon of parsley

1. Melt butter in pan. Gradually add flour, stirring until smooth.
2. Add milk and water, and stir over medium heat until boiling.
3. Simmer lightly for another five to seven minutes. Sauce should be quite thick.
4. Roll out pastry as thin as possible, but thick enough to fold without breaking.
5. Cut into four squares. Place fish fillet on each square and cover with white sauce and peas. Sprinkle with parsley.
6. Fold pastry over fish from both sides and stick together with a middle seam. Paint with egg or milk, and bake in oven at 200C (400F) for 30 minutes.

The Murray cod is a popular fish caught in the Murray River and its tributaries in south-eastern Australia. Though the word "cod" suggests an ocean fish. The Murray cod is very much a freshwater species. It may grow to 40 kg (80 lb.) or more in large waterways and streams. American substitution: Any game fish that grows to sufficiently large size to yield nice sized fillets.

Trout With Macadamia Nuts

4 trout. gutted. cleaned, heads on
Flour for coating
Freshly ground black pepper
60 g. (2 oz.) butter, for frying
Juice of 1 lemon
60 g. (2 oz.) macadamia nuts coarsely chopped

Coat fish with flour and pepper. Melt butter in pan. Add nuts and fry gently for two minutes.

1. Remove nuts from pan and drain on paper towel.
2. Wipe out pan and add another knob of butter.
3. When melted, add trout and cook gently for five to eight minutes per side.
4. Turn only once. Test for doneness; flesh should flake easily.
5. Place fish carefully on hot platter, and sprinkle with nuts.
6. Garnish with a few whole macadamia nuts, sprigs of parsley and thin slices of lemon.

Trout are found in many of Australia's inland streams. Macadamia nuts were first cultivated as a commercial crop in Queensland, Australia's north-eastern tropical state.

Tasmanian Devilled Rissoles in Cider

2 tablespoons cooking oil
1¼ kg (2 ½ lb.) game meat (kangaroo, emu), ground (minced)
1 teaspoon basil
2 tablespoons parsley, chopped
1 egg
⅓ cup beef bouillon or 1 tablespoon port wine in ⅓ cup water
4 tablespoons bread crumbs
3 tablespoons freshly chopped parsley, for garnish
6 tablespoons flour
Salt and pepper to taste
1 onion, peeled and sliced into rings
celery stalks, chopped
carrots, chopped
1 cup dry apple cider (alcoholic, of course)
½ cup beef bouillon

1. Lightly brown ground (minced) beef in cooking oil over high heat.
2. Reduce heat, add basil, parsley, egg and bread crumbs, stirring in bouillon (or port mixture) until correct thickness is obtained.
3. Remove from pan and allow to cool. Take large tablespoons of the meat mixture, form into patties and roll in 4 tablespoons flour, salt and pepper.
4. Lightly brown rissoles on all sides, then remove from pan.
5. Place vegetables in pan and fry gently until light in colour.
6. Add 2 tablespoons flour, stirring as you cook for one to two minutes.
7. Pour in cider and ½ cup bouillon, stir well and bring to boil. Lower heat, add rissoles and salt and pepper.
8. Cover and cook for 30 minutes, stirring occasionally.
9. Serve with parsley sprinkled on top.

It is widely believed that certain notorious "bush rangers" (outlaws) who escaped from the convict settlement in Tasmania early in the 18th century either ate or were eaten by the mysterious and frightening Tasmanian devil. The devil is now rarely seen and almost extinct. This recipe has survived with less-exciting game meat, especially those cuts that may be a little tough. The recipe also uses apple cider —Tasmania, Australia's island state off the south-eastern coast is known as "The Apple Isle." American substitutions: Bear or venison.

Galah Salad

1½ kg (3 lb.) galah meat
750 g. (1½ lb.) long-grain rice
½ cup French dressing
90 g. (3 oz.) butter or margarine
2 onions, chopped
125 g. (4 oz.) mushrooms, sliced
1 can whole-kernel corn
1 cup cooked peas
250 g. (½ lb.) cooked shrimp
½ red pepper, chopped
½ green pepper, chopped
125 g. (4 oz.) ham, chopped
4 tablespoons finely chopped parsley

1. Steam galahs until tender. Birds can be boiled or roasted, but the meat will be more tender if steamed.
2. Remove meat from bones. and chop into very small pieces.
3. Cook rice and drain well; mix in French dressing.
4. Melt 30 g. (1 oz.) butter (or margarine) in pan and sauté chopped onions until transparent. Remove from pan.
5. Add remaining butter to pan, sauté sliced mushrooms until tender.
6. Mix onion and mushrooms into rice. Mix in cooked peas, drained corn, shrimp, chopped peppers, parsley, chopped ham and galah pieces.
7. Mix together lightly and refrigerate.

About Galahs. The galah is a grey cockatoo found in many parts of Australia in large flocks. They wreak havoc on farmers' crops, but in many areas, they are protected. The flesh, when cooked. is a little tough and turns a dark grey. This doesn't matter in a salad recipe, however, in which the meat is cut up into very small pieces. This is a wonderful salad that uses rice and corn as the base, along with a little shrimp and other delicacies. American substitutions: pigeons or squirrel.

Nuggets Nardoo (Modern)

125 g. (4 oz.) butter
¾ cup brown sugar
1 egg
1 cup crushed pineapple
1 cup rolled oats
½ cup nardoo paste
½ cup plain flour
1 pinch salt
¼ cup chopped walnuts
1 teaspoon salt

1. Cream butter and sugar until light and fluffy, add egg.
2. Drain crushed pineapple well, add to mixture.
3. Stir in remaining ingredients until well combined.
4. You may substitute ½ cup flour for the nardoo, but of course it won't be the same.
5. Place teaspoonfuls of mixture on ungreased cookie tray.
6. Bake at 190C for about 15 to 20 minutes.

About Nardoo. Nardoo is a plant, native to Australia, found in the Outback. It bears edible seeds, from which the indigenous peoples made a paste or dough. It is said also to be an intoxicant. Nardoo is mentioned in many Australian bush ballads, such as that below which refers to Americans with the fond term (to Australians) of Yankees (no insult intended to Southerners, but Australians understandably see America as totally north relative to their own position on the globe).

No Yankee hide e'er grew outside such beef as we can freeze;
No Yankee pastures make such steers as we send o'er the seas--
As we send o'er the seas, my boys, in shipments every day,
From the far Barcoo, where they eat nardoo, a thousand miles away.
    --A Thousand Miles Away, Anonymous

Bush Angels

If you just happen to be trudging through the bush, and just happen to have brought along the following ingredients, you could make these outback desserts and late night snacks when you're telling yarns around the campfire.

    slices of bread
    can of condensed milk
    shredded coconut

In order to make this bush delicacy, you will need at least 1 grubby (i.e. sticky and dirty) child.

1. Have this chosen kid dip the bread in the sticky condensed milk, a part of bush cooking that only kids could enjoy.
2. Now, cross your fingers, and hope that the bread is not dropped on the bush floor (always dry and dusty).
3. Have your child press the milk-soaked bread in the coconut.
4. Toast over hot coals.
5. Insist that the child hand over the first cooked Bush angel to you (if it's clean).

Make sure the billy is boiling, and you can sip a cup of delicious billy tea as you munch on your Angels. How much closer to Heaven could you get? If you take a moment to forget your sticky fingers, you may look up at the huge expanse of the Southern Hemisphere (looks bigger than the Northern Sky of course). The sky is always clear, the stars twinkle without fail every night. The Southern Cross is there. Find an Aussie mate to point it out for you.

Kangaroo Tail Soup

1 kangaroo tail (about 1½ kg, 3 lb.)
2½ pints water
1 onion
1 carrot
½ turnip or small rutabagas
1 stick celery
90 g. (4 oz.) barley
1 teaspoon chopped parsley
salt and pepper

1. Wash the tail, trim off fat, divide at joints.
2. Remove meat from bones and cut into small pieces.
3. In a large pan, place bones, meat, salt and pepper, and barley and bring slowly to the boil.
4. Skim off fat just before and after boiling.
5. Prepare vegetables, dicing small. Add to the soup after it boils and simmer for 2 ½ hours.
6. Remove bones, add additional salt and pepper to taste.
7. Skim off fat if necessary, add parsley. Serve with crisp croutons. Aussies will take it with hot buttered toast.

Please don't visit Australia with the hope of shooting a kangaroo, not to mention eating it! It is true that in certain parts of Australia, the Northern arid areas, kangaroos are thought of as pests by some farmers. This is because they compete with farmers' cattle and sheep for that great scarcity in the Australian Outback: life-sustaining grass. Kangaroos are especially a nuisance because they tend to eat the grass down and into the roots, thus destroying the plant, making it difficult to regenerate. In these areas, kangaroos are not a protected species, although particular species (such as the Big Red) are protected and endangered.

Roast Rabbit

1 rabbit, skinned
3 slices bacon
4 tablespoons flour
salt and pepper
stuffing

Stuffing
½ cup bread crumbs
1 tablespoon chopped parsley
grated lemon rind
½ teaspoon salt
¼ teaspoon pepper
pinch nutmeg
1 teaspoon butter
¼ cup milk

1. Soak and wash rabbit. Make stuffing, insert in rabbit and sew up.
2. Rub with seasoned flour, lay bacon slices on top. Fatty bacon is better in this case, as wild rabbit flesh is very lean.
3. Place in baking pan with vegetable oil, cover lightly with aluminium foil, and bake 1 ½ to 2 hours at 190C (375F).
4. Baste every 15 minutes.
5. Serve with red or black currant jelly.

More about rabbits. Rabbits are not indigenous to Australia, so they are fair game. If you are stuck in the bush without any food (Heaven knows how you would get into such a predicament), a rabbit might just save your skin. They're difficult to catch, though, unless you have a ferret or a gun.

Roast Quail

quail
1 slice of bacon per quail
vine leaves
30 g. (1 oz.) melted butter
fried bread
red currant jelly
dried bread crumbs

1. To clean and pluck quail, see below.
2. Truss quail and brush with melted butter.
3. Place a vine leaf on the breast and on top of this, a bacon slice.
4. Secure with a strong tooth pick or skewer.
5. Cover lightly with aluminium foil and roast 1 hour at 200C (400F).
6. Baste frequently.

To fry bread

1. Heat oil to very hot, as for French fries; drop in squares of day old bread.
2. Quickly brown and remove, so that it remains crisp.
3. Serve quail on fried bread, spread with red currant jelly.
4. Top with gravy sprinkled with dried bread crumbs.

Quail are found in most parts of Australia where they nest in long dry grass. They are a tiny fat bird (a relative of the grouse). Their flocking together when disturbed is remarkable.

To prepare quail: Do not scald bird, as the skin will break. Pluck feathers from one side, holding bird by leg, then by wing. If feathers are difficult to remove, pour boiling water over difficult part. Cut head off, place bird on breast and cut slit in back of neck, pull neck out and cut off close to the body. Cut between vent and tail, pull out entrails with fingers. Chop off legs above the knee joint. Rinse out inside of bird. Substitution: Cornish hens one finds in the supermarket.

Jugged Hare (outback, sort of)

You need a large "jug" or jar in order to prepare this unusual dish. One is not likely to have such an implement in the Outback. But you never know, you may just happen on a lonely homestead a couple of days after you catch the hare.

1 young hare
One 2 cm slice of bacon
3 sprigs of thyme
1 onion
pepper and salt
¾ cup flour

1. Skin and clean the hare, and hang it head down for 2 days (1 day if it's too hot to sit out in the sun).
2. It would be best to do something to keep the blowies (flies) away from it while hanging.
3. Take a large wide-mouthed stoneware jar. Place hare in jar,
4. Cut bacon into small cubes.
5. Add bacon, onion, thyme, salt and pepper.
6. Make a smooth paste with flour and add to hare.
7. Add more water until hare is just covered.
8. Cover jar with cloth or aluminium (called al-u-min-ium by Aussies) foil, and place in a saucepan of hot water.
9. Boil for 3 to 4 hours, depending on size and age of hare.

To skin and gut a hare or rabbit: To skin the rabbit, cut through the skin at back of the rabbit's thighs. Force your fingers inside of the skin and pull it off towards the neck. Once down to the neck, cut off the head. To gut the rabbit cut around the neck, and make a small incision under the tail. Open hare's mouth as wide as possible, and force fist down gullet, keeping two fingers pushed out front. Retract and extend fingers once or twice to loosen insides. Push hand further into hare's gullet until index finger reaches tail. Force finger through small incision and curl around tail. Pull tail through incision and grip in hand. With other hand, push down strongly on head of rabbit. With a strong flicking movement across the knee, pull hare inside out. Remove entrails. Just joking. If you really want to do it yourself, do a search on YouTube and you'll find a video showing you how.

Crocodile on the Barbie

2 crocodile steaks (100 g. or 4 oz. each)
fresh ginger, finely chopped
fresh peppercorns, ground and whole
garlic, finely chopped
2 teaspoons macadamia oil
90 g. (3 oz.) bunya nuts
3 teaspoons wattle essence
30 ml (2 oz.) chicken stock
30 ml dry(2 oz.) white wine
200 ml (8 oz.) cream
chives

1. Grind half the peppercorns, amount to taste.
2. Coat crocodile steaks with peppercorns, garlic and ginger, seal in plastic wrap or other container, and leave overnight in refrigerator.
3. Cook on barbie at medium heat, turning two or three times during cooking. In a hot pan, lightly fry the bunya nuts until brown, then add wattle, stock, cream and simmer until thickened.
4. Serve sauce over crocodile, and garnish with chives.

About Bunya nuts. These are large seeds from Australia's native pine tree which grows in northern New South Wales and Southern Queensland. Regular pine nuts available in most stores these days could be substituted.

About wattle. There are over 1,000 species of wattle plants in Australia. These beautiful plants, some of which are the size of shrubs, others large trees, produce clumps of small bright yellow flowers in spring (October). Wattle essence is obtained from one of these species, and is now available in most Australian food stores. It is very unlikely that one could find it anywhere in the United States. We suggest trying a substitution of either oregano or bay leaves.

Damper

flour
water
butter
jellies and jams
honey or golden syrup
(Aussies only)
salt
a green stick

Damper is a traditional scone-like bread baked over or on the camp fire. The trick is as much in the cooking as it is in the mixing.

Prepare a cooking fire by allowing a camp fire to burn down to a heap of red coals. Select a green stick, about 1 m. long, that is straight and about 2 cm thick. Try to get one that doesn't require chopping down a whole tree.

1. Place flour and salt in mixing bowl, add water a little at a time until a thick dough is formed. Keep the dough as stiff as possible. Knead well and allow to sit for an hour or so.
2. Roll into a long sausage shape, then twist around the green stick so it resembles the doctor's emblem of a serpent on a staff.
3. Place stick with damper over fire. The easiest way to cook this damper is to rest the stick on one or two forked sticks, so you don't have to hold it all the time.
4. Turn the damper over every now and again. The most important thing to watch is not to cook the damper too quickly. It may take an hour or more.
5. When cooked, remove from fire and break damper from stick.
6. Serve pieces smothered with butter, jam, jellies or honey.

Black Jelly Bean Damper

Prepare dough as above. Knead into a flat disk, then sprinkle with black jelly beans. Roll up into a ball, place at side of fire, and allow to cook slowly in the embers. If the fire is slow enough, you can leave the damper to cook for 1 to 2 hours. Dough may be also wrapped in aluminium foil and tossed in the smouldering fire..
Variations. Use any other flavour jelly bean, of course. Instead of jelly beans, enclose an egg inside the dough. It will be nicely cooked when you retrieve the damper.

Billy Tea

Many of the rules of tea making described earlier apply to making billy tea. However there are a few differences. First, you must have a "billy." This is a large can-like metal container, with a wire handle attached to the top. This is not very functional because when the billy is boiling, it's very hard to pick up—the wire handle hangs down close to the fire, and against the hot side of the billy. It takes a little practice to thread a strong stick, or your hunting knife under the handle so you can lift the billy off without burning your fingers.

1. Prepare a hot, but small fire. Place the billy ¾ full of water on the flames. A black soot coated billy is better, as it heats more quickly. (How you carry it with your other things without getting black all over you is your problem).
2. When the water is boiling, remove the billy from the fire as quickly as possible, and immediately add about 6 teaspoons of tea (English Breakfast Tea—nothing fancy), depending on the size of the billy. Usually, allow 1 teaspoon for each cup of tea to be made.
3. Do not return the billy to the fire. Leave to the side to keep hot, but do not allow to boil. If the tea boils it will taste like bitter soup.
4. Now is the time for the tea to "draw." It is best left to sit for a few minutes. There are various beliefs about how the drawing process may be speeded up. Some advise taking the billy by the handle and swinging it forcefully and evenly round and round over one's head. This does seem to work. However, we have also seen the billy fly away from the handle several times when swung over the head. A gentler way is to tap all around the sides of the billy with a teaspoon.
5. Pour tea as reported in **cuppa tea**. Milk should be added first. When drinking tea in the Outback, one never drinks from a cup and saucer. An enamel mug is the traditional container, though not very functional, because it conducts the heat so fiercely that one can burn one's lips very easily.

Bush variation: Some hardy Outback types claim to drink billy tea flavoured with a gum leaf (leaf from a eucalyptus tree). If you decide to try this, choose a sweet smelling tree, and break only a tiny piece of leaf (1 cm at the most) into the tea while it is drawing. It is best to drink eucalyptus tea without milk.

About eucalyptus. It is widely believed that eucalyptus trees have medicinal value. Eucalyptus oil is sold everywhere in Australia for the treatment of cold symptoms.

The Australian's love of billy tea is expressed in this bush ballad:

You may talk of your whisky or talk of your beer,
I've something far better awaiting me here;
It stands on that fire beneath the gum tree,
And you cannot much *lick it—a billy of tea.
So fill up your tumbler as high as you can,
You'll never persuade me it's not the best plan,
To let all the beer and spirits go free
And stick to my darling old billy of tea.
And at night when I camp, if the day has been warm,
I give each of the horses their **tucker of corn,
Then the fire I start and the water I get,
And the corned beef and damper in order I set,
But I don't touch the **grub, though so hungry I be,
I wait till it's ready —the Billy of Tea.
-- *The Billy of Tea*, Anonymous, about 1840.

*To "lick" someone or something is to win or do better than. It does not usually mean to give a beating as in American usage.
**"Grub" and "tucker" mean food.

Eggs 'N Oranges

This recipe will not work with Emu eggs. You need chook (hen) eggs.
  hen eggs
  large oranges
  salt and pepper

1. With a sharp knife, cut out the top of each orange, making an opening big enough for an egg.
2. Scoop out the flesh then insert the egg.
3. Prepare a slow fire with plenty of glowing coals.
4. Make small holes in the coals and place the oranges with eggs in the coals.

The heat of the fire along with the juice still left in the orange skin, will actually boil your egg. Depending on how hot your fire is, remove egg in orange when cooked (usually about 7 minutes). This is a great way to get kids to cook eggs.

Variations: Many quick-cooking foods may be prepared in this way. (1) If you would rather avoid the orange flavour, find a flat rock with a depression, not too hard to find in a creek bed. Clean it off, place over a very hot fire, and when hot, break your egg into the natural pan made by the depression in the rock. The egg will cook right before your eyes. Or, cut a hole in a slice of bread, lay on hot flat rock, break egg into hole. Of course, the standard practice of enclosing the food in wet clay then placing this on the fire is also an effective way to cook. Depending on the clay, though, you might need a hammer to break it open once it has baked. (2) Attach a green vine or wet string to a safety pin, stick pin through shell of egg, and suspend egg over fire until cooked. Sounds crazy, but it works! (3) Encase food in banana skins and cook the same as in oranges. (4) Onions may be substituted for oranges. (5) For dessert, core apples, fill with raisins and sugar. If they will fit in orange cases, cook as above, otherwise, coat with clay and cook.

Fried Tiger Snake

Tiger snake
herbs, preferably chives
salt and pepper
cooking oil

Tiger snakes, one of the most poisonous snakes in the world, are only found in Australia. They are named because of their distinctive yellow and brown stripes. They are not large snakes, as snakes go. The largest would be about 1 m. Most are about ½ m or less, and the thickness of a hot dog. If you are bitten by one, you've probably had it, unless you can get to a hospital for an antidote right away. You are strongly recommend that not to go hunting for one of these nasties, just so you can try out this recipe. In case you are foolish enough to track one down, here's how to do it.

Actually, Tiger snakes are rather timid, and will not attack you unless you happen accidentally to stand on them. If you make a lot of noise walking through long dry grass in summer in a field populated by Tiger Snakes, you can see the grass swirling, and hear the swishing as the snakes speed away from you.

The way to catch one is to leave food, especially sugar, around your camp. This is no surprise, is it? It's the same way you can catch a bear (or for it to catch you!) in North American forests.

Old hands claim that the best way to kill a Tiger snake is to use a pliable long wire that will, with a strong flick of the arm, crack down on the snake's back and break it. By far the most effective way is to use a long forked stick to push down on the snake, pinning it to the ground just behind the head. If you are an experienced bushman, you will be wearing strong boots, and with the heel of such boot, bring it down on the head and crush it. It helps to have a mate do this, or hold the stick down for you. If you follow these directions you will have yourself a dead snake, though it is believed that the Tiger snake, no matter what you do to it, never dies until sundown.

To prepare Tiger Snake

1. With the snake definitely dead, cut off the head.
2. Draw the knife down the belly from tip to toe (so to speak).

3. Dip the snake into boiling water, then work the point of the knife under the skin at the neck, and loosen the skin all around.
4. Roll back skin, have a mate hold body of snake at neck, peel skin completely off.
5. Remove entrails (not much to remove) or leave and discard after cooking. Cut into sections.
6. Heat oil in old bush frying pan until quite hot.
7. Quickly fry snake until golden brown. Do not overcook, or meat will be tough. (It's tough anyway.)
8. Serve sprinkled with chopped chives or parsley. If you can find some wild asparagus (sometimes found along the edges of irrigation canals) boil and serve also.
9. Salt and pepper a must.
10. Potatoes (regular, not yams) baked in the fire's coals go nicely with this dish.

Frankly, even though they are poisonous, we'd rather Tiger snakes weren't killed. They're part of Australia, after all. And by the way, they are a protected species!

Baked Freshwater Eel

Although Australia has a dry climate, there are many small rivers and creeks that run in winter and spring. They are teaming with freshwater eels, as well as other freshwater fish. Eels are included in this chapter because they are the easiest to catch. As for fishermen everywhere, a plentiful supply of beer is needed in order to snare these creatures, usually very late at night. When you hook these eels, you will think you have a shark on the line. They fight to the death, often tearing their bodies off the hook in order to get free.

Prepare as for Tiger snake, above. Prepare fire and hot plate as for Witchetty grubs, (next) but do not have fire quite as hot. Roll pieces of eel across hot plate. Depending on type of eel and where you caught it, flesh may be quite fatty. Cook until fat has run out. Serve with baked yams.

Singed Witchety Grubs

Witchetty grubs (from the Aboriginal *witjute*, the name of roots in which the grubs are often found) are various larvae that feed in the wood of eucalyptus trees, most often between the bark and the trunk. They are about 2-4 cm long, with a fat creamy body about the width of a man's thumb, and stumpy legs. The Australian indigenous peoples who live in the Outback are said to consider them a delicacy.

witchetty grubs
an old piece of metal
salt and pepper to taste
a little cooking oil (optional)
yams

1. So you're stuck in the Outback without anything except a little salt and pepper! The Outback is desolate often without vegetation, but one is sure to find somewhere a scrap piece of metal left from some failed effort to drive an enormous distance, or maybe from a Mad Max movie set.
2. Scrub the metal clean, hopefully in a little sand and water from a nearby trickling creek.
3. Prepare a fast, trench fire and place the metal across the top.
4. Immediately place yams in coals beside the fire.
5. After about an hour, when the hot plate is very hot, drop the witchetty grubs down and rapidly roll across the metal plate.
6. Keep rolling until they are browned all over.
7. Remove from heat, allow to cool.
8. Remove yams from coals. Break open yams and serve each yam with a witchetty grub nestled in the middle.

Grub is a word used by Australians to refer to any larvae found in the garden and elsewhere.
About Yams. Yams are a type of sweet potato cultivated in many parts of Australia and the South Pacific generally. If preferred, ordinary potatoes could be substituted, and cooked in the same manner. Another substitute is pumpkin.

Bunyip Buns

The Bunyip is a mysterious animal, probably a bird (the experts say the Australian Bittern), far more mysterious than the Tasmanian Devil, which has been sighted only by the most experienced Outback bushmen. They are mostly sighted late at night, during fishing trips with a bunch of mates and a case of beer.

The Bunyip is a diurnal animal, but is so well camouflaged (it not only changes colour, but also shape) that it is difficult to distinguish from the greys, browns and whites of ghost gums (a particular type of eucalyptus tree, made famous by the Indigenous artist, Albert Namatjira). It is also a cowardly animal, and has been known to hide behind other animals when it observed the barrel of a hunter's gun.

Nothing is known of its reproductive cycle, except the one thing that makes it possible to share this recipe with you. It establishes nesting places made of a strange fibrous substance, rather similar to the truffles dug up in northern Italy. In fact, it is possible to find these Bunyip nests using small piglets, properly trained. One must be very lucky to find Bunyip hollows. Although Bunyips are sighted mostly where ghost gums grow, one cannot be sure that bunyip nests will be found in the same place. Furthermore, it is claimed by some old timers that Bunyips systematically destroy their nests every few days—or at least move them to other places—in order to fool would-be nest farmers.

2 cups plain flour
1¼ cups milk
¼ cup sugar
1 egg
1 teaspoon salt
60 g. (2 oz.) butter
1 packet yeast
1 Bunyip nest

1. Mix yeast with a little warm milk and sugar, add rest of milk (warmed) and let stand 10 minutes.
2. Rub butter into flour until it looks like oatmeal, then add sugar and salt.
3. Wash and drain Bunyip nest well, removing any pieces of fur or feathers that may be attached.

4. Clip off any black pieces—these are old and bitter. A fresh nest will be a rich brown in colour and will have a smell similar to that of fresh cut grass.
 5. Break in pieces, place in blender and grind. Add to flour mixture.
 6. Add yeast mixture and beaten egg.
 7. Mix with wooden spoon, and work into soft dough.
 8. Knead well, then make balls of dough about half the size of tennis balls and place on greased cookie tray.
 9. Cover with damp dish cloth and leave in warm place until dough rises to about double the size.
10. Boil a little sugar with one cinnamon stick in water, and glaze tops of buns.
11. Bake at 215C (400F) for about 20 minutes, or until golden brown.
12. Serve hot with butter, sprinkle with sugar and cocoa, or powdered hot chocolate.

Glossary of Indigenous Australian Foods*

Bugs. Not the insect kind. Term given to primitive looking lobster like creatures found in the bays and inlets of Australia's north eastern coast. Look something like a lobster tail with eyes and no claws. A somewhat stronger taste than lobster.

Bunya bunya Nuts. Australia's own pine nuts, from Australia's native pines. Unless bought commercially, must be boiled for at least 30 minutes.

Bush cucumber. Tastes like a cross between regular cucumber and melon, with maybe a touch of grape.

Bush tomatoes. Said to be a relative of the commercial tomato and potato. Dried and ground, can be a substitute for paprika.

Emu. The great Australian flightless bird, resembling the ostrich. Now farmed commercially. The meat is red. The eggs have a strong flavour, and are equivalent to about 10 chicken eggs.

Eucalyptus oil. A well known oil, now marketed even in the United States as a cold remedy. Distilled from Australian gum (eucalyptus) trees. Be sure to use food grade oil. It's very strong.

Finger Limes. ("lime caviar"). Grows in subtropical and dry rain forests in North Eastern Australia. The lime has a prickly shell that encloses a pulp that may be of varying colours, including green, yellow, orange, red, purple, black and brown. Used as garnish for sea foods, wet salad, or on ice cream.

Kangaroo and wallaby. This game meat, as with all game meat, is low in fat. Steaks are popular, as are smoked and dried "jerky." This, you can buy at souvenir shops and airports in Australia.

Kakadu plum. A green olive size plum very high in vitamin C (some say the highest). May be found manufactured into a jelly.

Kurrajong flour. Made from the ground seeds of kurrajong trees. Makes a tasty spread mixed with macadamia nut oil. As a flour it adds a nutty flavor to breads.

Lemon aspen. This is a small yellow fruit found in Australia's eastern rain forests. Can be used as a citrus substitute.

Lemon myrtle. Tastes a bit like lemon grass. Bake into breads or herb butter. Available commercially at specialty stores in Australia.

Munthari. These are small apple flavoured berries, that grow on creeping plants found among the dunes of South Australia. They are about the closest Australians have to cranberries.

Nardoo. A plant bearing edible seeds from which the Aborigines used to make a paste or dough.

Native mint. There are two edible native mint bushes, with very strong flavour. Recommended for use in sauces such as pesto, or bunya nut butters.

Native pepper. Various plants yield leaves that a pepper-like quality. Look for Mountain pepper, Dorrigo pepper, or Snow pepper in specialty stores (in Australia, that is).

Quandong. These are a kind of native peach, with a touch of tart apricot. Very popular in Australian country kitchen for jams and jellies. Widely available in Australian supermarkets.

Water chestnut. The Australian species is the same as that found in Asia.

Warrigal greens. A wild spinach is found around Australian inland waterways, and a version of this was used by Captain Cook to fight off scurvy in the 1770s. They are also sometimes called, in the Sydney area, Botany Bay greens.

Wattle .There are about a thousand species of wattle (ranging from trees to shrubs) in Australia. One species produces seeds that are edible, once roasted. Now widely available and promoted in Australian specialty shops, and some supermarkets. Use in pasta, ice-cream, breads and even beverages.

Wild Tamarinds. A bright yellow and orange fruit, depending on the species. Good for sauces and dressings.

Witjute grubs. (witchetty grubs) These are the larvae of large moths which lay their eggs in particular wattle bushes. Popular for soups, but, may even be roasted. Has a nutty, peanut butter flavour, and a pork like texture.

Yabbies. Small lobsters found in Australia's fresh water streams.

Yams. These are tubers grown in tropical areas. They have a very short shelf life, and thus are not often commercially available. Highly nutritious substitute for potato, and have much more fibre.

*Much of the information in this glossary drew heavily from *Uniquely Australian: A wild food cookbook*, by Vic Cheriloff. Bush Tucker Supply Australia. 1994.

Aussie Measurements and Ingredients

Oven temperatures

Many of the recipes in this book date from a period when ovens did not have temperature settings. They were wood, coke or coal fired ovens, and the measurement of temperature was done by experience, putting one's hand in the oven, adjusting the size or fuel of the fire. Typically, the recipes used expressions such as "hot" "moderate" or "low" for oven temperatures. I have translated these rough measures (and Fahrenheit where indicated) into Celsius throughout the entire book. For your convenience a conversion chart is below, although you can find such charts freely on the Internet. Please note that these can only be rough estimates and that they may also vary slightly according to whether your oven is gas or electric.

	Fahrenheit	Celsius
Very Hot	450	230
Hot	425	220
Quick/Fairly Hot	400	205
Moderately Hot	375	190
Moderate/Medium	350	175
Warm	325	165

Weights and measures

All measurements in this book have been converted to metric. Many of the old recipes of course used various versions of "imperial measures" of ounces, pounds, pints, fluid ounces etc. Many also use teaspoons, tablespoons, cups and fractions thereof that also do not translate exactly into American usage. A tablespoon in America is different from the Australian or English tablespoon. Measuring cups in America do seem to differ slightly from measuring cups in Australia. I have tried to make accurate conversions, but nevertheless many such conversions can only be rough guesses. The following charts have, in most cases, guided the conversions. The charts are based on those provided in the PWMU (Presbyterian Women's Missionary Union) cookbook widely used in Australia.

Imperial to metric

Imperial	Metric
1 oz.	30 g.
4 oz. (¼ lb.)	125 g.
8 oz. (½ lb.)	250 g.
12 oz. (¾ lb.)	375 g.
16 oz. (I lb.)	500 g. (½ kg.)
24 oz. (1½ lb.)	750 g'
32 oz. (2 lb.)	1000 g. (1 kg.)

US butter weights	Ounces	Grams
1/2 cup	4 oz	113.4g
1 tablespoon	1/2 oz	14.2g
1 teaspoon	0.02 oz	4.7g
1 pound	16 oz	450g

Imperial liquid to metric

Imperial liquid	8 oz. cup Imperial or Metric
2 fl. oz.	¼ cup
2½ fl. oz.	⅓ cup
4 fl. oz.	½ cup
5 fl. oz. (¼ pint)	⅔ cup
6 fl. oz.	¾ cup
8 fl. oz.	1 cup
10 fl. oz. (½ pint)	1¼ cups
16. fl. oz.	2 cups
20 fl. oz. (1 pint)	2½ cups

Cooking terms and ingredients

Australia	USA
Self-rising flour	Self-raising flour
Corn flour	Corn starch
Castor (caster) sugar	Confectioners' sugar, fine sugar
Mince meat	Ground beef
Chuck steak	Braising, stewing steak
Main dish	Entrée
Golden syrup	A very sweet extract from sugar cane. And no, it is not molasses. No equivalent in the US. The closest might be dark corn syrup.
Vegemite	A vegetable yeast extract from a by-product of beer making, no equivalent in the USA. Similar to the British Marmite, but this is a beef extract.
Custard Powder	Hard to find in USA. Makes making custard very easy. Essential for some cookie recipes.
Biscuit	Cookie
Scone	Like, sort of, what is known as a soda biscuit. But it's nothing like the scone you get in Starbucks.
Icing sugar	confectioner's sugar, powdered sugar.

Also by Colin Heston

9/11/TWO
This gripping novel offers a glimpse into the real world of counter terrorism, hints at why 9/11 was allowed to happen and warns us that it could easily happen again. It's politics as usual in New York City when Larry MacIver, world renowned criminologist, is tapped by NYC Mayor Ruth Newberg to save NYC from a second 9/11 attack. Will it be nuclear? Will it be bio? MacIver and his geeky assistant Manish Das must overcome FBI ineptitude, CIA intrigue and, most of all, the evil and ruthless Iranian terrorist Shalah Muhammud, to save the city. In the underground of this story, so suspenseful, so frustratingly funny at times, are the crucial questions of counter terrorism that worry anyone within a couple of hours drive from New York City: Will it be a drone next time? Will New York politics doom the city's defences? Written before drones were widely in use, the novel seems prescient of much that has happened (should and should not have happened) in the world of counter terrorism.

Miscarriages
Teen Chooka grows up in the weird world of 1950s Aussie pub life. When his alcoholic dad dies, he searches for his identity, and that of his shadowy underage girlfriend, Iris. Captivated by the pub's many crazy customers and their raucous stories, Chooka becomes a boozer just like them. But Iris, after a miscarriage, disappears and Chooka sets out on a search that takes him to foreign places including Melbourne university and Vietnam. The search ends in a Melbourne pub, where they start over, but this time there's a different ending.
"...a brilliant, unforgettable book about real people...a sensitive, touching and poignant story." - *Reader's Favourite.*

Ferry to Williamstown
In this raucous Aussie story, corpses pop up in the Yarra river while Lizzie entertains her powerful and kinky clients in her Winnebago, parked on the ferry to Williamstown. Tightly bound Detective Striker, confronted by the mob of Catholics, wharfies and communists who rule Williamstown, struggles to solve the mystery. Lizzie gets engaged to her uncle Bobby, the lame ferry driver, and her mum, Babs, spellbound by the strange Father Zappia, tries to solve her own mystery of St. Robert's toe. She throws a raucous send-off party for Lizzie, and out of the chaos emerge many truths.

Holy Water
In this very naughty, hilariously irreverent farce, Alphonso, a Mexican drug lord, captures the market in Holy Water, acquires a university for his LGBTQ daughter, and makes an Australian cardinal the pope. "...a

well written and humorous comedy story that will suit fans of surreal plot twists and anarchistic humor." —*Readers' Favorite* .

About the Author

Colin Heston is the pen name of a criminologist of international repute. He was born in Australia and spent much of his professional life in New York, writing academic books on crime and punishment. In his role as criminologist he has written and edited many books, including a four volume encyclopedia, *Crime and Punishment around the World,* and most recently, *Civilization and Barbarism.* He currently resides in Anglesea, Victoria Australia where he writes fiction, as he looks out over the beautiful Anglesea rive, and cooks authentic Aussie dishes. Heston's previous fiction includes *9/11 Two*, in which criminologist Maciver tries to thwart a terrorist drone attack on New York City, *The Tommie Felon Show,* A collection of stories ranging from the absurd to the improbable, *Miscarriages* a coming of age novel about Australian pub life in the 1950s, *Ferry to Williamstown*, a comic mystery yarn set in 1960s Melbourne, and most recently, MONA, an updated edition of *The Tommy Felon Show*, and *Holy Water* a satirical farce about a Mexican drug lord who corners the market in Holy Water..

HARROW AND HESTON
Publishers

AUSTRALIA, NEW YORK & PHILADELPHIA